A Writer's Notebook

A Writer's Notebook

Anthony Powell

WILLIAM HEINEMANN: LONDON

First published in the United Kingdom in 2000 by William Heinemann

1 3 5 7 9 10 8 6 4 2

William Heinemann
The Random House Group Limited
20 Vauxhall Bridge Road, London SW1V 2SA

Random House Australia (Pty) Limited
20 Alfred Street, Milsons Point, Sydney, New South Wales 2061, Australia

Random House New Zealand Limited
18 Poland Road, Glenfield, Auckland 10, New Zealand

Random House South Africa (Pty) Ltd
Endulini, 5a Jubilee Road, Parktown 2193, South Africa

The Random House Group Limited Reg. No. 954009

www.randomhouse.co.uk

A CIP catalogue record for this book is available
from the British Library

Papers used by Random House UK Limited are natural,
recyclable products made from wood grown in sustainable
forests. The manufacturing processes conform to the
environmental regulations of the country of origin.

Typeset in Bell by
MATS, Southend-on-Sea, Essex

Printed and bound in Great Britain by
Mackays of Chatham PLC, Chatham, Kent

ISBN 0 434 00915 6

THIS NOTEBOOK IS DEDICATED WITH LOVE TO
HARRY AND HOPE COKE
GREAT-GRANDCHILDREN
OF
ANTHONY POWELL

Introduction

It is only by internal evidence that I can put an approximate starting date to this *Notebook*, though the evidence is not in itself conclusive, or, indeed, consecutive. Situations, and suggested names for characters, develop almost of their own volition. I find, however, on page 3 a name used in my first novel, *Afternoon Men*, which leads me to suppose that the *Notebook* was begun about 1930.

The next definitive date is 1934, the year in which I read aloud my work in progress – *Agents and Patients* – to the girl who was to become my wife. We were, coincidentally, staying in her family's Westmeath home. We sat on a window seat in the library. The view over park and woods, with hills beyond, made an incomparable background for courtship.

Feeling the utter impossibility of writing a novel

while in the Army, my attention was focused on the book that was to be *John Aubrey and His Friends*. But names, situations, and quotations which took my fancy continued to be jotted down in a battered 'dummy', relic, of my publishing days.

As an example of erratic juxtaposition, the name Widmerpool is first mentioned in the *Notebook* above the view of a room seen through the wall of a bombed house. When *A Dance to the Music of Time* came to be written, Widmerpool at once appears, advancing through the fog. The sight of a bombed room, its elaborate plasterwork still intact, only makes its point four volumes later.

Increasingly, throughout the *Notebook*, Shakespeare became my companion, his point of view ever more congenial.

Finally, I would like to thank my wife, who read the manuscript book onto tape, and also Helen Gould who typed it.

The family of Anthony Powell wish to thank John Saumarez Smith and Alan Bell for help and advice concerning this *Notebook*.

Notebook

'This the staple of the World's great trade;
On this soft anvil all mankind was made.'
(Rochester).

'Ye who listen with credulity the whispers of fancy
and pursue with eagerness the phantoms of hope;
who expect that age will perform the promises of
youth, and the deficiencies of the present day will be
supplied by the morrow, attend to the history of
Rasselas Prince of Abissinia.'
(Samuel Johnson)

Publisher talking: 'I understand he has written a
book of the bitter-sweet variety.'

'Yet seemed it winter still, and you away.
As with your shadow I with these did play.'
(Shakespeare, Sonnet XCVIII)

'FIRST GUEST: I am so bored I can knock my head
against the wall . . .'
(Chekhov)

An unattractive woman makes an improper joke,
which only causes embarrassment.

Old Colonel X lives in a very small house in the
country, but wears loud checks and expects to be
treated as the squire. He has a pretentious son who
fails the Diplomatic Service, and goes on hanging
about at home.

The evil old mother dies, and is discovered in her
chair by the guests, when they return in fancy dress.

An old man in a rage takes out his false teeth and
brandishes them.

Assignations in the London Library.

A publisher who wears a green shade over his eyes.

'Some dwarfs and doubtful creatures sat here and there, lolling out their tongues, pinching each other and behaving oddly enough.'
(Aubrey Beardsley, *Under the Hill*)

'Now come tidings of weddings, maskings, mummeries, entertainments, jubilees, embassies, tilts and tournaments, trophies, triumphs, revels, sports, plays, then again as a new shifted scene treasons, cheating tricks, robberies, enormous villainies in all kinds, funerals, burials, deaths of princes, new discoveries, expeditions, now comical then tragical matters. Today we hear of new lords and officers created, tomorrow of some great men deposed and then again of fresh honours conferred. One is let loose, another imprisoned, one purchaseth, another breaketh, he thrives, his neighbour turns bankrupt. Now plenty, then again dearth and famine, one runs, one rides, wrangles, laughs, weeps, etc.'
(Robert Burton, *The Anatomy of Melancholy*)

Overheard: 'I never liked the last inmate, there was always a strong scent of *Fougère Royale* about him, though I must say his choir discipline was excellent.'

I mustn't distract you as I see you have reached the exciting part of your book (*Ulysses*).

They had to hang all their Matisses in the servants' bedrooms.

I should like to meet writers who really count, like G. K. Chesterton, Belloc.

Names
Sfumato
Lilias

Rabbit's blood on my leather coat, a woman says.

Aut Sousa, aut nihil.

Utrillo or Uccello.

An Academy picture of Philip baptizing the eunuch.

Mauger, a butler; Lord Strathinvert; Lord Uttoxeter.

She wrote in a large untidy hand, like that of a vicious child.

The clocks in this house were always wrong.

A young man lives with a woman of forty, and is kept by a girl of his own age. Later the girl also falls in love with the woman.

A very modern vicar has been reading *Punch* aloud to me.

The choir is so important, it teaches the boys *esprit de corps.*

What was always a mystery to me, when I was at school, that men, who could have made a fortune merely by walking across the stage of a music-hall, should have preferred to eke out a livelihood by teaching little boys, but no doubt they had their reasons.

I read in the *Daily Mirror* that an ex-policeman has become a priest.

On the telephone yesterday I thought you were the footman.

Don't you adore the *Daily Mirror*?

One of the men they sent me was quite alarmingly witty.

Incense and Insensibility, an Anglo-Catholic Oxford novel.

She's only fifty and dances divinely.

What do you do to get exercise in London? I find that if I catch a train as soon as I leave the City, I can get down to Brenchley in time to put the weight for an hour or two before dinner.

For goodness sake don't put me next to a girl who has just got engaged. I always see them mentally comparing one to their fiancé.

The insincere face of the butler.

Name: Lord Boteaux.

I shall never forget how George Fawk introduced old Lady B as his wife to the Portuguese Minister.

We played bridge until 3 ack emma.

Lord Salaman
Landscape with Ruins } titles for books
Naughty Figs

A young man, who's anxious to get rid of his mistress, says that it wouldn't be very nice for him if she became one of the girls who sit about in the Café Royal.

'The Christians came, their lewd profession taints, unlearned, unchaste, uncharitable saints.'
(Horace Walpole)

'Uncouth rhyme.' Gray.

Mrs Nunnery.

'Can I claim worst disgrace on manhood fall?
Be born a White-head and baptized a Paul.'
(Charles Churchill)

As a practical joke he once gave the butler a safety razor blade instead of a tip, and the butler cut his hand on it.

When I was a lad, a jolly fellow would go out and get tight, and have a woman, and know he had had a damn good time. Young fellows aren't like that now.

The hungry forties, the roaring forties.

He scratched the seat of his trousers moodily.

Their faces deformed with manliness.

'But she the while was murmuring low:
"If he could know, if he could know
What love, what love his love should be!"'
(William Morris, *The Earthly Paradise*, part 1)

Names
Peregrine
Torquil
Festus
Ferkin

Dignity and Impotence.

J'aime mieux une vertu commode qu'un vice fatigant.

Congreve said that he could never look at a monkey without very mortifying reflections.

Ah, you're buying experience, young man.

I suppose, being an artist, you meet lots of interesting and amusing people.

Souvent femme varie, bien fol est qui s'y fie.

A homosexual middle European baron:
'I haff a castle in Transylvania.'

A girls' school in the neighbourhood of Hell Fire Bottom.

You must meet my nephew some time, he has just come down from the BBC.

You have, of course, a village idiot?

An American princess who has married a black prince.

A is taken to a strange flat in Paris by a friend who leaves him alone for some time, extraordinary people come in, and the flat is being done up by workmen.

'Pity is the intelligent anticipation of our own troubles to come.'
(La Rochefoucauld)

A young artist comes to stay in the village, he has a love affair with one of the daughters of Mrs N, he goes on staying, and the affair gradually drifts until they get heartily sick of each other. She asked him to use the house as much as he likes, with the result that he is never out of it, but takes no notice of the owners. Eventually, she falls in love with him.

The vicar practises Black Magic.

While a girl is walking in the country with her lover they come upon the female village idiot with the butcher's boy.

'I am not a highbrow, I don't go about saying how marvellously Galsworthy writes, or gushing over Orpen, but, when I look at a sunset, I do see that there is something in all that sort of thing.'

Two girls talking: 'Of course we could always just live with a man without getting married. I don't know that I should like that very much somehow.' 'No dear, of course not, neither of us would.'

They discuss mineral waters as people do wine.

Courtly old bores.

The Pleasance, the home of the Fosdicks.

Count Torboni
Baron Rathany } foreign noblemen

"By the way' said Sir George, 'my wife sometimes takes a fancy to guests, she sees so few, you mustn't mind.' Sir George Overmantle. Of course when he married her everybody called for miles round to see what she was like, but he wasn't a bit grateful. He stood in the drive with a shotgun, and said that the only reason he had married the woman was to be free of the neighbours.

Of course it's practically impossible to get rid of one's vicar.

She was left with no money, and three sons to educate. One became a clergyman, but the others did very well, one being a gossip writer and the other in the City.

'May I present Mr Zouch,' said Torquil. 'Mr Zouch, the Marchesa d'Agramonte.' 'Mr Zouch, I am glad to have you know me,' said the Marchesa as they shook hands. 'Torquil here will fix you a highball.' 'Mr Zouch,' said the Marchesa, 'say no more, Mrs Nunnery is a great little old lady.' Torquil Fosdick moves slowly across the skyline on his penny-farthing bicycle. Torquil gives a cocktail party and the imbecile family play their hurdy-gurdy.

Two great cowards have a quarrel, and almost come to blows.

An inn run by a stockbroker, who has been in prison – for Bohemian weekends.

A novel of London life called *Goddesses, Maidens and Queens*. At times the thought had haunted him to make an automaton of bronze . . .

The American princess attacks Z, who sleeps with her maid.

Rogeras de Feronage or possibly de Firange.

X who had been blackballed from some of the best clubs.

Literary agents, gossip writers, professional seducers, philosophers, thaumaturges.

'To my mind there is nothing so illiberal and so ill-bred as an audible laugh.'
(Lord Chesterfield)

'Do you mind if I speak plainly,' said the supposed Colonel. 'Yes,' said Oliver, 'I should hate it.'

'Isn't it funny,' said Susan, 'the way one person is always more in love than the other.'

There was an elderly man who looked as if he might have held a commission in the Rumanian Army Service Corps.

An expository treatise, and a critical examination of international agreements, for the unification of granio-metric and cephalo-metric calculations, together with some directions for collecting information and opinions for anthropometric measurements to be made on living subjects for physical anthropology.

A is having an affair with B's wife, and tries to teach her habits of punctuality, so that B too shall profit in some way from the situation.

She was the sort of woman who, if she had been taken in adultery, would have caught the first stone and thrown it back.

'What would you quote me for Chinese?'

It is considered a quite sufficient condemnation of a book, for a reviewer to say that similar events have never happened to him.

Lesbians are the only really feminine women left.

With the exception of the Headmaster of his preparatory school, X had never seen so depraved a face.

After a hundred lovers women have still drawn no conclusions about life.

A mistress always sounds such a pompous thing to have.

He likes flogging dead horses and live women.

Dignity is one of the rarest qualities in a woman. Just as for males, pomposity is only too common.

She wrote badly, even for a lesbian novelist.

A foreigner: 'You joke?' X: 'I joke.'

An author who allows himself a good deal of platitude.

Immovable forces and irresistible bodies.

Name
Hector Mattlebury.

Being a professional beauty is, after all, more a question of the temperament than of looks.

The Pope's hard bargain.

Summer contacts.

'What are you laughing at, Rose?'
'Thoughts,' I said.

Half the vice of the world is due to the collector's instinct.

'I once went to a nightclub in South Kensington.'
'Is that so?'

X appears to be on very intimate terms with a woman Y and makes Z very jealous. Z cannot see that X is really in agony, because the intimacy between him and Y is over.

Nothing is so humiliating as to be liked for the qualities one hasn't got, and women always do it.

A girl nags at her young man, because he won't fight another man who she thinks has insulted her.

Two lovers quarrel, and later in the evening meet at the same restaurant.

A daily woman says, 'It's a lovely day for the Armistice.'

A country house, discomfort, some guests go sightseeing. 'I'm afraid there isn't room for you,' says X's hostess.

Nicephorus Calistus recounts that the Persian magicians, in order to bring our religion into bad repute, caused an evil and disgusting stench to emanate from the place where Christians were.

Medicines.

A man, depressed about a love affair, gets drunk at lunch and loses himself in a maze.

Story opens in a photographer's studio.

Name
Scrub

Wisecracks for Demi-vierges: title for book.

X sat backwards in a chair, as if he was going to give a lecture, or playing a game.

An unpleasant child.

X gets a bill for a present, bought long ago, for a woman with whom he has now quarrelled.

A girl, after being kissed by a man, says, 'Are we engaged, darling?' The man says, 'No, we are not exactly engaged . . .'

A beggar playing Rubinstein's Melody in F on a violin.

The rise and fall of the leaf, finds out them with weak chests.

Rooms in winter.

A man looks at a photograph of himself, and is discovered.

A rich woman pretends that she is kept.

X says, 'I take dull examples on purpose.'

Names
Count Vladimir (Lipseus)
Pantamelion

X falls downstairs on his way at night to his mistress's room.

A sensible-looking girl, dressed in velvet.

The Irish: We hear a little less about them, etcetera.

'It were the Bulbul; but his throat,
Though mournful, pours out such a strain:
For they who listen cannot leave
The spot, but linger there and grieve,
As if they loved in vain!'
(Byron, 'The Bride of Abydos', canto 2)

You can do anything in Fleet Street, except make a friend.

The story opens with a girl looking through a French window at her mother.

Gigolos talking about history.

A man explaining yachts to a tart.

Chapter beginning: The dwarf passed out about five o'clock.

Name
Fosdick

Soldier describes the plot of *Loyalties* or similar play.

Someone who insists on reading the paper aloud.

A man takes a friend to a favourite restaurant. The friend makes a terrible scene, so that the man cannot go back there.

A guest at a country house does not realize that he is sitting next to the governess, and embarrasses her and his host. Later he discovers.

Two girls who live in the country, one of them hearty, the other ex-chorus girl, young man falls in love with the former girl, until awful mother falls in love with him.

Dinner at the Xs'. Host talks all the time. A lodger trying to write a thesis in the same room.

A man trying to transact an important piece of business is disturbed by two boys who want to take his photograph.

X says: He is not like an ordinary parson. Did you know he said 'because I am in a dog collar, etcetera'.

He was one of those people who are taller when they are sitting down than when they are standing up.

'Livery stuff,' said X, finishing the bottle of sherry.

'Peg to hang dreams on.'

'Hikers.' 'Hikaz,' said the Major, pronouncing the word as if it were Arabic.

'What's wrong with you,' said X, 'Do your feet hurt?'

The parson makes nonsense of the lesson when he reads it.

A young man has a romantic night with his mistress, but in the morning a workman arrives at a very early hour.

We can't all make good, can we?

X said, 'I can't really say I know him, he once tried to kiss me in the passage, fortunately he was not tall enough.'

People play cards with a child to amuse it, and quarrel with each other because they lose.

A man quarrels with another man, in a nightclub, because he feeds his dog.

Lesbians writing poetry in an album.

Strong men wept.

A man makes a drawing of another man in a café.

Head waiter at Neubabelsberg. 'You've a fine character Mr H etcetera', 'his clothes' 'not a waiter tonight', collecting vouchers for an aeroplane journey to Munich.

We have to fight our own little battles.

A man half kills a wasp and watches it thoughtfully.

A hunchback being sick.

Two men share a flat, one reads the other's diary, it becomes a vice.

Names
Keen
Winn
Freddy

The chambermaid at the hotel had a brother-in-law who wrote novels in the style of Pierre Loti. He found it difficult to place them with a publisher; it seemed that he had written three novels in this style, and none of them had been placed yet.

A man explaining something intellectual to a girl very carefully; she said, 'Wait a minute, I must listen, they are playing so and so.'

Bechhofer Roberts and Trevor Allen.

The defeatists.

Casanova in England, Tommy etcetera.

'We thought of the FO, or the BBC. You know there is no exam for that.'

Some women seem to imagine that one has nothing better to do than to sit up all night listening to anecdotes about their first husband.

Title for a short story: 'The Woman Was Not a Type'.

I envy you your height, you could wear very loud checks.

X is offered a lift by a friend in love with her, but says, 'Thanks, I would love to, but my doctor says I must walk.'

Short story. A man has an affair with another man's wife, owing to this he rescues the husband from death. After that the wife falls in love with the husband.

I must go off now and see a man who is blackmailing me.

'Shall I sing "Frankie and Johnny"?' 'No, anything but that.'

Hilary Stratton, Oliver Derwent-Wood. The Gog and Magog of Chelsea boredom.

Novel opens with a long account of tying-up scene behind Shaftesbury Theatre.

'I might come in and have a drink with you.' 'You might come in; a drink depends on my hospitality.'

Names
Minhinnick
Reith

Showing prospective tenants over a flat.

A letter to the Income Tax official (harassed husband?).

The snobbery of loving fat women.

A tart says, 'Don't you want a good time dear?' X says, 'No, not if I have to pay for it.'

'Easy to draw but hard to get.' A loaf of bread by pavement artist.

Peasants are always so middle-class.

A man who is forever saying that his student days, when he had no money, were the best in his life.

'Je deteste les femmes.'

X stepped aside to avoid a man carrying a sandwich board inscribed with the words, 'The wicked shall be turned into hell.'

'Happy days are here again.'

A bottle of Jordan Water.

A man is in bed with a woman, another man comes round early in the morning about a matter of business, and flirts with the woman.

A turns into a gallery to avoid a bore, and is followed in there by him.

'By bogland, highland, down and fen,
All Englishmen, all Englishmen!
Who with their latest breath shall sing
Of England and the English spring!'
(John Davidson)

Have you ever tried going to bed early and alone?

A man tells another man in his cups what he thinks of his painting.

Names
Teape
Mrs Mendoza
Cattermole

'*C'est beau de voir ce bateau; ça coupe l'horizon.*' Heard in a cocktail bar.

'*Il faut travailler; il ne faut pas bâtir des châteaux en Espagne, comme nous disons.*'

'*Enfin Hollywood est un peu shocking, mais on passe dessus.*' Girl overheard on a French bus.

The Atrocious Orgies of the Spanish Clergy (book title seen).

C'est sérieux, c'est moderne (a garage).

An actress says, 'I don't know anything about pictures, but you know I always instinctively pick out the right one. Is Bach a good composer? You see I don't know. He is? Well I like him, it's funny isn't it?'

X says, 'I can't afford to be seen about with a girl of whom people say, "Why, aren't you a nice brown colour".'

'I shall deprive women of myself,' a man says.

Drinks on the house.

For the sake of argument.

A man goes away with a tart to get a collusion divorce, and falls in love with her.

Name
Chipchase

'He's got—' Mr X lowered his voice.

The great thing about adventurers is that they never have adventures.

He was one of Nature's co-respondents.

It's the thought that counts.

Name.
Chummy.

Good hunting, gentlemen.

An elephant never forgets.

A man makes a hole in a newspaper to watch people opposite, in a railway carriage.

Two medical students: 'The first time I saw an operation, etcetera, just like a piece of meat . . . take gallstones for instance.'

Local monochrome.

Surely you RAF men have a wife in every airport.

Name
Lord Coleporter
Greek fire

He was killed playing croquet.

Name
Puckering

'Down in the saltmarsh, heaving a cutlass.'
(T. S. Eliot)

One of the most touching things about the rich is how good they are to each other.

He was with a woman who looked old enough, but by no means ugly enough, to be his mother.

A man examines one of the legs of his sofa before a girl comes to see him.

'I cover the waterfront, I'm watching the sea.'

Not tonight, Josephine.

A publishing firm called Snooper & Busch.

'Have you met my little wife? 'Yes, I should like to meet her again.' 'So should I.'

X sits watching this with the fixed unbelieving expression of a sceptic at a séance.

'I suppose you despise me for being so dumb.' 'On the contrary, I would like enough money to get even half as dumb as you are.'

At a party, make up your mind whether you are going to go all out for women, food or drink. You can't have all three.

I can never see why mean people should not be pitied, it is just as painful for them to part with money as it is for the poor.

Names
Bloodworth
Scoby

An Indian regiment, ——'s Horse.

X looked like a very poor imitation of a woman, or a rather brilliant one of a man.

He shot himself waiting in Cook's.

Being Irish is like being homosexual, it gives the speaker a permanent topic of conversation.

'What is the house like?' 'A ruin.'

Name
Commander Venables

'Ickle', woman's nickname. A very modern granny. Burning children with fireworks by accident.

Name
Chipchase

They were sacred in Egypt (cats).

Scene in a painter's studio while he is at work.

'He that is not free is not an Agent but a Patient.' (John Wesley)

Americans: to the last generation typically unconventional people, to this typically conventional.

A woman writes obscene words on the walls of an empty house, to work off her inhibitions.

'Artistic studies, they were.'

English woman followed by a very small Spanish soldier. 'Who's your friend?' 'I don't know, we have been some way together.'

Names
Pimley
Pemberthy
Members
Heropath

He was the most pathetic of figures, an Englishman who has gone Scotch.

Mr Bailey (Curiosity Shop)

Colonel Packe (a friend of my father)

A wedding in the Guards' Chapel.

A story about publishers considered. Two men who dislike each other a great deal are left together as literary executors of the work of a dead author. Book ends with one getting religious mania, and parading the streets with a banner.

'Do you drink vodka, Count?' said Princess Maria. And these words had once dispelled the shadows of the past. (*War and Peace*)

'Of course if you like peasant types.'

'Was Hemingway that man who wrote a book on bull-fighting? *Life in the Afternoon.*' 'For me bull-fighting is little more than a lot of fat men in fancy dress ill-treating a cow.'

The more repulsive of the two speakers, they were both odious, paused and turned round.

'I always stare at women,' said X; 'It's a bad habit I picked up in Spain.'

He is a typical Viennese juvenile.

Some scenario writers discuss the age of one of their number.

An American, garrulous without being chatty.

A voice like a ventriloquist's doll.

One of the reasons that films are so bad is that producers assume that a class of picture-goer exists, stupider and slower witted and more vulgar than themselves, which would, of course, be impossible.

'In ancient years,' says the old man, 'in the time of the worthy patriarchs I should have chopped him to pieces at the stake, but nowadays its all darkness and rottenness.' (*The House of the Dead*)

Sir Fat, a Chinaman.

'It looks like our diesels are giving trouble, I guess it's a bum mixture.'

Restaurants: Au pied de Svengali, Chez Mithridates, The Casanova.

A tough director who falls for a baby film star.

'He hasn't got a sausage.'

'He stank like Abraham.'

'Tearing about half a dozen cat houses in half.'

These are my jewels.

'The Zanie of Columbus'. (Milton, *The Apology for a Pamphlet*.)

What do you think about things in general?

La race féline (in a tree).

Une vraie chemise de Nessus.

'When desire takes you by the throat, old boy.'

Idly throwing a pebble in the direction of some children who, with fanatical fury, were attempting to enclose one of their number in a box intended to hold cricket stumps.

Drawbridge, a butler.

Someone describes *Anna Karenina* as a book all about a woman in Russia who leaves her husband.

An American says, 'You must meet X, he's a very real person.'

A man carrying a portrait of himself.

General at Sunset ⎫
Stockbroker in Sandals ⎬ titles for books

Names
The Wise Child
Widmerpool

Elaborate mouldings of a room seen through a gap in the wall when the house has been bombed.

The only positive thing about him was his Wasserman test.

'I take women as I find them,' said X, 'the latter is usually more difficult to achieve than the former.'

'What I say is if dollars could have won the war, the indigestion merchants would have won it long ago.' Heard in a pub.

'I worry too much. Shakespeare's dying words.'

Some men going to a funeral discuss the corpse. Opening of a novel.

Making love is always a complicated and somewhat unsatisfactory business. Anyone who is prepared to pretend that it is a simple, straightforward matter is always in a strong position for having sexual success. Just as one finds that state authority is necessary, but should be kept as much as possible in the background, one feels that love is necessary but that love, as opposed to all its concomitants, should be stressed as little as possible in an explicit manner, to safeguard its fragility.

It is one of the virtues of the Welsh, as opposed to the Scots and the Irish, that they are at great pains to explain their own failings as a race. This does not mean they are not sometimes unpleasant, or the reiterated self-praise of the Irish and Scots means they are pleasant.

Most men would want to be thought the sort of man who has a lot of women, but taking the men who have a lot of women, as a whole there are not many one would wish to be like.

A civil servant: His most intimate moments, one felt, were to the burden of 'you may wish to comment' . . . 'passed to you for action' . . . 'we concur'.

There is nothing like being happily married for getting a woman down.

You should treat whores as duchesses and duchesses as whores. I find the former goes better than the latter.

Blackhead, a civil servant ... German some generations back, his room, cups of tea and paper bags.

Trudget, a civil servant. Two large blue hands lying on the table as if they were waiting to be cooked. Gaukroger, Liddament (query FO), Horrobin (*names*).

'Do the French diplomats have mistresses?' 'The Italians are worse.' Overheard in a bar.

Twenty-six-hour week, if necessary longer (minutes).

Of all the arts, music seems to be the one which worldly people find most tolerable to occupy themselves with, without disturbing their worldly activities and ambitions.

General and porridge.

Batman at Matlock (soldier servant).

Colonel Hogbourne, 'Eric' . . . Derek,
revelations when censoring.

An attractive man, yes. You won't get a woman
away from an attractive man. The question is how
to get her away from a dull, stupid, and boring man.

Colonel X and Colonel Y never allowed their eyes
to leave each other's faces, like an engaged couple.

A senior officer fixes his eyes on the black buttons
as if pondering the pageantry of the regiment.

The passage smelt as if camels had been stabled
in it.

'After that I was Feathers to him.' (MI 17)

A man sits wrapped in gloom after conversation
with a bore.

X says, 'I have just had a terrible experience with
an AT.'

Women have a way of saying 'Oh yes', when a man's name is mentioned, indicating that they have slept with him.

The Name and Fame through Afghan Passes (Colonel Carlisle's favourite book)
Bradders in Finland
Lucky Alphonse

I shouldn't think a woman could ever really forget a man with breath like his.

The strength of the Jews lies in the despair of those who know they will not be left in peace.

Behaviour misunderstood, by not realizing that someone is in love with someone else.

'As to baths, I shouldn't think he overdid it.'

Russians have nothing to lose but their chains, there is not one that pulls properly end to end of the Soviet Union.

Idols of the tribe (Bacon's *Novum Organum*).

One of the very few realistic advances that can be achieved in life is to realize that one has been an ass regarding a given subject.

A man who has dodged the war says that he was doing something more or less like being in the Resistance Movement.

A literary man with no manners and no conversation.

An egotist says, 'Some people don't like me, others fall under my spell.'

'A woman's problem is how to have power without giving pleasure.'

A Question of Upbringing
The Furies   } book titles
The Valley of Bones (Ezekiel)

The awakened concubine: sad concubinage.

Dickens was lucky enough to get his blacking factory over early in life.

A walking race.

Widmerpool takes great trouble to make an introduction, and then refuses to allow the two people to talk to each other.

'Those children's voices made me mighty sad.'

'Send him a no-can-do,' said the General, 'Send him a no-can-do,' and he went on repeating that.

Names
The Lofts of Chelsea
Lord Bridgnorth

'In the Resistance?' 'The sales resistance I suppose.'

The change from D. H. Lawrence's view of marriage, saying 'Any two people who like each other' (Denny).

In quarantine for a hangover.

The best things in life are free.

Names
Isbister
Grimsby

'Let Powell, house of Powell, rejoice with Synochitis a precious stone, abused by the ancient sorcerers.' (Christopher Smart, *Jubilate Agno*, XXVII)

A man who makes a register of old Etonians in English fiction.

Straining at ATS and swallowing camels. X, because he wants to kiss a girl has to kiss her sister or another woman, too. X's girl is not surprised, the other woman is astonished.

Names
Stringham
Steven
Mablet

Bridget's cold house.

The tailor his loud checks came from, and dud cheques went to.

A man says with horror, 'Later I saw him without a hat.'

A hospital Christmas isn't what it used to be. Why is it? In the old days there were always two obstetricians dressed as Father Christmas, and the housemen as animals.

Life as Russian billiards: the gate goes down — everything double.

A literary critic says, 'It's rather exterior.'

'If every woman is at heart a rake, every rake is at heart a woman.' 'You must tell that one to the bishop, he would like it.'

Name
Weedon

'The OR (Official Receiver) is a wonderfully good scout.

Titles
A Matter of Taste
Titles to Symphony
His only Genius Title was *A Title to Sympathy*

Like many people of his sort, he was ill at ease in the presence of memories of the past.

The dreaming spires of her course in psycho-analysis.

A rather bouncing man is absolutely broken doing some dreary job in the Army.

X usually walking about with two squash rackets in their presses.

Name
Peplow

All his geese are Swanns, in fact some of them are Charluses. (Brightman)

In spite of what is said to the contrary, men of action tend to be woolly-minded, and imaginative people clear-minded.

Centurion's Luck, i.e. for a great sum I purchased that citizenship (but it was the Chief Captain who is recorded as doing this in *Acts*).

Book title
Proper Stations

Gentle Bulgarian rain was falling.

Being unfaithful to a woman gives a man rather tender feelings about her, but a woman usually hates a man when she is being unfaithful to him.

An Army Encamped
Fragment for a Bacchanal } book titles

Having no opinions is a positive advantage for a literary critic.

He expects one to remember every stroke he has made in polo during the whole season.

'I don't know whether she was a shop girl or a princess,' said X, speaking of a girl he picked up on Wimbledon Common. 'Almost certainly a princess,' said Y.

The intellectual arrogance of clever people, intolerable as it often is, is nothing to the intellectual arrogance of ignorant people.

Name
Lord Trowbridge.

Self-love is so often unrequited.

Names
E. St John Grimthorpe, a novelist.
Lady Edward Wentworth.

Wishing well: 'Do you have to wish?' 'You can please yourself.'

Parents are sometimes a disappointment to their children; they turn out badly.

There is a lot of truth in the typical melodramatic situation of Cavalier falling for Puritan maid or vice versa.

The Floors of Parquet

The hostess said, 'It's a horrible party, I know I am going to hate it.'

Opening of a novel: 'I often used to talk to Barnby about women . . .'

It is an illusion of every woman that she is less tiresome than other women.

The business of tiresome and egotistical people always knowing when it would be unwise to do their stuff.

People like the rich for their money but not for what they can get out of them? Begin a section with this thought.

A novel: *Whistling Women*

Some sort of a description contrasting the will and the imagination from its scepticism, perhaps seen in terms of two people.

'Blow, blow, thou winter wind,' said Mr Deacon.

Name
Mrs Drum

Widmerpool walked beside the Minister with a file under his arm. He had the expression on his face of a dog carrying a newspaper in its mouth.

In military life, as in love, anxiety is a predominant feeling.

Names
Horace
Roland
Roderick
Gwatkin

'When Roland brave, and Oliver,
And every paladin and peer.
On Roncesvalles died!'
(Scott, *Marmion,* canto 6)

Jenkins' girl, Jean, leaves him with a book inscribed with quotation, Apollinaire. *'Je suis soumis au chef des tiges de l'automne.'*

Mrs Fitz's brothel.
The Cavendish.

Sir Gavin Walpole-Wilson quotes Flecker. 'For lust of knowing what we should not know, we take the golden road to Samarkand.'

A house called Hill of Dreams.

One of the great points about people who have an eye to the main chance is that their interest in one cannot fail to be acceptable, because it is of necessity flattering.

Name
Craggs

A feeling of power-seeking men for pretty girls.

X says, 'economics are politics.' Y replies, 'it always seems to me that if anything politics are economics.'

Friends of the rich.

Widmerpool is last seen walking away into the fog.

Priapic grapple.

X says, 'I have always so looked forward to being old.'

Sillery gets a peerage in the end.

Castano's *'bella posizione'*, speaking of Russian billiards.

A Buyer's Market

X says, you may be quite sure that women like you for your bad qualities.

'Did you hear Brightman's remark about Sillery's peerage?' 'What did he say?' 'A pity there would be no heir.' 'He is witty.'

The strange thing about middle-aged and elderly people is not that they do change, but that they don't.

Love has been written about so much that it is almost impossible to think of it subjectively, although the exact reverse seems to be true. Because someone shoots themself for love they are not necessarily more in love than someone who does not take violent action.

The approach of winter. It is a great conviction of youth from which some people never escape that everyone is having a better time than they are, but dining with Widmerpool, etcetera.

Years later Barbara Goring says, 'I thought Tompsett was so wonderful.' 'Did you?' 'But I thought you were wonderful too.'

Short eventually reminisces about sentimental times at Oxford.

Name
Greenham

A literary paper, *Perimeter.*

People do not mind how much they are interfered with. What they cannot stand is being treated as adults.

For the end. Stringham goes to live with Miss Weedon. Baby Wentworth commits suicide.

The mystique of 'getting on' as opposed to the real practice of it.

Clearing up the mess after the death of Uncle Giles, enema and his Army Commission etcetera.

Widmerpool sacks Truscott from his Donners-Brebner job.

When Jean makes some intellectual remark to Jenkins, it seems a piece of incredible intelligence, because he is in love.

The two opposed methods of rich families, e.g. Villiers or Astors.

Like all museum officials, he regarded himself as an Adonis.

Tokens of affection.

Like many successful politicians, he had the face of a rather gross schoolboy.

Pageboys at the Ritz: 'It's General de Gaulle in there.' 'Give me news not history.'

Women don't like men, they like looking after men.

Someone said they knew no better definition of hard work than taking decisions. In that case no work is harder than an artist, because this entails taking decisions all the time.

Life is a comedy for those who drink, and a tragedy for those who eat.

Old Boy dinner with Le Bas, organized by Widmerpool. ?After the war.

Women are so self-conscious that any woman who seems unselfconscious appears attractive, but she thereby lays herself open to the suspicion of self-consciousness.

People always admire ruthlessness.

Gratitude has some claims to be regarded as the rarest of human virtues.

There is nothing people find harder to understand than indifference to any given matter.

The point of a love affair, lying to some extent in the memory, i.e. something pleasant at the time, finally turning sour or vice versa.

The Courts of Love (Book title)

The extraordinary cunning of women.

Love of power in people is often associated with hatred of authority.

'And yet I wondered whether she would ever leave my dreams.'

Two lovers; Today was happy until luncheon.

An older woman describes some man as not very attractive, and Jenkins' heart sinks.

Question. Jenkins goes to Kensal Green to see Mr Deacon's tomb, and comes back by Portobello Road, and meets Gypsy Jones driving a car slowly through the street, with peace slogans, circa 1951.

For Love or Money (*Book title*)

That hearty, natural egotism, so different from the furtive kind, perhaps is preferable to assumed modesty.

The beauties of yesterday become muttering, mad old women.

To be loved is intolerable to the true Narcissus.

The margin between success and failure is a narrow one, Uncle Giles etc.

Names
Boggis
Stileman

Widmerpool plays croquet in uniform, refusing to relinquish some papers from under his arm in a brief-case.

'There is nothing sadder than a happy marriage,' said St John Clarke vindictively.

'Unmade friendships are like unmade beds,' said St John Clarke.

Marriage is a subject about which it is very hard to get accurate information.

Unburned Boats (*Book title*).

Quiggin marches in a left-wing procession.

The Acceptance World (*Book title*).

The horrible conceit of human beings is that they understand each other.

The stage at which people like or dislike the criticism of their friends.

Professional seducers, although in one sense the most egotistical of men, also sometimes tend to develop an anonymity that makes them acceptable to women.

The Ufford is used as an HQ or Ministry (?Foreign Secret Service) during the war.

People always talk of a love affair as if lovers spent all their time in bed.

Although unintellectual people should not be allowed to be rackety, rackety types have a link with people of the intellect.

The way in which different people are exemplified for coping with emotion.

The consummate egotist does everything negatively, i.e. the other person is to make the suggestions, particularly women.

A novel begins: 'My wife, an orphan, has five brothers. Hilary succeeded to the title and lives quietly in the country,' etcetera.

Acceptance . . . signifies an engagement on the part of the drawee to meet the bill in money when it falls due. Crump, *Banking*, p.117.

Names
Udall
Cordery

'So this is the famous Widmerpool hospitality we hear so much about.'

'Curse your charity.'

Somebody discusses absolute values.

A book, *The Heart is Highland*.

It wouldn't pay for the sticking plaster round my heart.

He spent his time boasting about how much his shoes cost, and showing off in front of the children.

In the break-up of a marriage he would take the side of the partner with the most vitality.

Hearing Mrs Patrick Campbell read 'High Tide on the Coast of Lincolnshire', and not being able to eat tea after (circa 1898).

The Officer: 'He committed suicide in the bathroom. I heard say, I was not informed.'

The really extraordinary thing about professional seducers is the drivel they talk, there is not a single cliché they leave unsaid. That is why they have such a success with women.

I wished him luck in the Acceptance World. ?Last sentence of book.

I saw them coming up the street together looking like Culture and Anarchy.

The Isbister Retrospective Exhibition – Sir G. Walpole-Wilson, and Sillery.

Mrs Widmerpool turns up at the Ufford.

A man who has no temperament.

'All blessings are mixed blessings' (St John Clarke).

Eleanor Walpole-Wilson, ATS Officer of Widmer-pool's girl, an ATS driver.

Lady Anne Stepney marries Sir Magnus Donners, and becomes a hostess.

An artist is almost always something of an embarrassment to his work.

'He was always a dreamy boy.' (?Members)

A great deal of individual success in life is based on not having the slightest idea what other people are like.

The mysterious feeling of looking through a ruined doorway (?a bomb site).

'Rides like a monkey sitting on a commode.'

?Members becomes an RC.

A mixture of aggression and timidity with women.

Love affairs when you are young consist largely of finding out what you yourself are like.

If you describe women in a book there is always a moment of 'most wonderful girl you ever met, old man', or alternatively 'something out of a fashion paper.'

He had been faithful to his wife only in retaining the unshakeable belief that she could not have her leg pulled.

The Warminsters (*Book title*)

There is nothing more demoralizing than habitual truck with under-production.

'Buck House'.

Noises in radiator.

'The keyhole in the door,
The keyhole in the door,
My Christ I saw her do it through
The keyhole in the door.'

Templer eventually marries a serious intellectual woman?

A man says to another man, who has just kissed his wife, 'Aren't you going to kiss me too?'

The Ardglass mansion in Northern Ireland during the war.

'You don't have to pay women to sleep with them, only to stop.'

Rosie Manasch married Jock Udall, son of Lord Brentbridge, press lord.

She clasped together her pink plump little hands delicately moulded and caught in as if by elastic bands at the wrist. With popping eyes Rosie stood on tiptoe as if to emphasize the solemnity of the married state.

A way in the Army in which one man's active life can be geared up to achieve some insignificant job.

'Women always think that if they have knocked a man out, they have knocked him out cold, but he sometimes gets up again.' (Barnby).

At the beginning of the Second War men thought themselves lucky to get into uniform at all.

It is a tradition to depict Generals as stupid men, and it must be admitted that this is sometimes just, but there are many exceptions.

The Army is at once the best and the worst place in the world of egotism.

It is a common illusion that the Army is in some way different from other institutions, notably in its own peculiarities. Strong-willed Privates and weak Generals.

Names
Pugsley
Jeavons
Updyke

I had known Warminster by sight at school when he had been called Erridge. I met him first oddly enough through Quiggin at the time of the Spanish Civil War.

'Rot,' said X. 'Dukes are much more cunning than Earls.

All men may be brothers, but thank God they are not all brothers-in-law.

I am an only child, accordingly there has always seemed to me something rather sinister about large families.

It is not the sensual woman who has lots of affairs, it is the unsensual one.

'Eyes are windows of the soul,' said St John Clarke, 'but the blinds are usually lowered.'

Different Opinions (*Book title*).

Di, Di, in a collar and tie,
Quizzing the girls with a monocled eye,
Sipping her hock in a black satin stock,
Shooting her cuffs over Pernod or bock.
Clad as a matelot, she can't get fat a lot,
Bringing her trim little craft into dock,
Like a torpedo in brogues or tuxedo,
She's tramping around at Cape Cod or the Lido,
From Bournemouth to Biarritz, the fashion parades,
Welcomes debonair Di in her smart tailor-mades.

Amorous, glamorous, something too clamorous.

I want to dazzle Lady Sybil.

As we rattled on towards the tomb.

Titles: *Spalding, Sleaford, Thrubworth, Monkseaton. Dogdene, Sleaford house.*

Melancholy is the curse of the upper classes.

An Oxford figure who talks about travelling: Sykes, Codrington or Byron.

Widmerpool describes the meaning of his name.

'I think I'll just comb some of the lice out of my hair,' says a very smart girl.

The horror of telephone boxes.

Intelligent people's capacity to learn.

Jenkins pays a visit to a country house with his wife.

Jenkins meets Erridge, now a left-wing peer, Lord Warminster, with St John Clarke.

Jean's hands.

That summer I found I had thought of Jean less.

There was room at the inn, but no room at the bar.

I have always held that an honest clubman is the noblest work of God.

Umfraville turns up in the war as an RTO.

F Mess housed all but the lowest dregs of the Divisional Staff.

Dicky Umfraville sings 'Molly the Marchioness'.

Widmerpool's resemblance to Pepys.

One of the manias of contemporary aesthetic doctrine is for what is called originality.

Looking at the Vermeer book with Kronaker during the Blitz.

Duke of Wellington says something of the first Earl of Warminster: 'Why shouldn't they make him an Earl, he's not such a fool as Combermere, or such a rake as Anglesey.'

Cadena College.

'He was that little noisy MP who dresses like a pimp.'

Names:
Bloodstock
Udney (?Courtier).

'I nearly had kittens when those men wouldn't stop talking to you.'

Jenkins sees Widmerpool on the steps of a TA Hall before the war.

Eleanor Walpole-Wilson in the war says to Jenkins, 'Why hello, Nick, you have got some grey hair.'

Exhibitionism in various people takes different forms.

A Virginia Woolf whistle.

Religion is the final materialism.

'A man who writes down all the things he knows about his friends': Quiggin.

Jenkins thinks of when Jean first met Duport.

A title: *Lord Plynlimon.*

The Huntercombes' Ball. Their Van Dyck, which turns out to be a Dobson.

A Buyer's Market

There is a great difference between people who are ambitious and people who are fascinated by ambition.

Ted Jeavons gets tight and talks about 'the officer' (First War phrase).

Labour foreign policy, *New Statesman,* September 34, October 34, Peace ballot.

Jenkins has a discussion with Jeavons in a nightclub. Jeavons is drunk and talks about the upper classes. 'If you were the only girl in the world.' 'I always feel rather sorry for your generation.'

A man who, for a bet, ate a dozen, cut off the joint and two veg, was sick at the seventh when someone lighted a cigarette, but tried again and succeeded. (reported by Ted Jeavons).

"There was a certain anonymity in aristocracy." (Proust)

'Lor,' cried Mrs Boffin, 'what I say is, the world's wide enough for all of us.'
'So it is, my dear,' said Mr Boffin, 'When not literally – But when so, not so . . .'
(Dickens, *Our Mutual Friend*)

A man in the Secret Service, who is writing a novel in the style of James Joyce, which is stolen by foreign agents.

Although there was nothing of which my Colonel disapproved more thoroughly, we had to come in contact from time to time with the Secret Service, and this officer, with whom I had to deal, happened to be an old acquaintance.

On a course during the war.

'Throw your money about, young man, I expect it's the Governor's.'

The Army is of necessity the world of the will; if the will is weak then the Army is weak.

Hypnotism by some individual exercised upon other people.

Children of the Jockey Club.

In Lady X entertaining Matilda and Rosie Manasch, one saw the dregs of Holland House.

'Here is the Security Directive.'
'Read out any funny bits.'

Man of Aran, New Gallery, April 1934.

'She kept a tame rat.' 'How typical.'

'You must see my coloured photographs of the Dutch bulb fields.'

A bad divisional headquarters is the scum of the earth.

Jeavons in a nightclub. Jeavons and tart.

'He ran a pin in Gwendoline, in Lower Grosvenor Place.'

A capacity for being silent without being shy is a great social weapon.

I don't want to change my metabolism.

A peer who hums cowboy melodies.

That admiration for the Army, which in England is found very rarely.

There is one rule without exception. If women want to break off a love affair they always do it in the most brutal manner at hand.

Women may sometimes show some discrimination about whom they sleep with, but they will marry anybody.

'People will say that they (the smart X family) are absolutely charming if they offer you a second cup of tea.'

'No, old boy, it's a poem.' (?Stringham)

'Gossip binds the upper classes together.'

Utterly unconscious of his own failure to charm. (Stringham says)

(Stringham says): 'Feel shocking this afternoon, had too much lunch, red in the face, self-inflicted wounds of course.'

One of the cardinal points of X's life was that anything he wanted he had to have; he could therefore never admit a woman was beautiful unless he had slept with her etc., i.e. that the only reality is action.

Molly Jeavons says, 'I don't think that such and such a face powder is any good.' X says, 'What have I to do with it?' Molly Jeavons said, 'Somebody said you used it and your skin is always very good.'

Personal charm, Mr Deacon used to say, has unfortunately nothing to do with personal altruism, or, indeed, any other virtue.

In the War Office somebody says, 'I am going into my dad's office when I leave this school, he's got some jolly pretty typists.'

It is extraordinary how much certain people set up to be good, and how little others do, and what a small margin exists between the two sorts.

Somebody says something, in 1939, about Fat Boy Gort (the General).

The Plungers, old-fashioned name for the Tins (Life Guards).

At Lady Molly's (book title).

A rich man explains to a poor one how much more spending money the poor man has.

Spider, Mona's original seducer, turns up in the Army.

Erridge is killed in the Spanish War, his younger brother in the '39-45 War, and they have to sell the house.

It is curious how unwilling even the most insensitive people are to be branded insensitive.

A bore talks about racing and bloodstock (see Duke of Portland's memoirs).

A Yearling Sale at Newmarket.

Intelligent people do not like having to defend weak intellectual positions, which politicians have to do all the time.

Title: *Lord Tenterden.*

People who are not naturally good are much better at being bad.

The less in love you are, the better you are able to handle the situations of love, which of course explains the success of Don Juans, who are never in love at all, except with themselves.

A discussion about heraldry in an air raid? A man in the War Office who talks heraldry.

The Terms of Reference

How far is the prevention of exports of arms to Bolivia and Paraguay effective? September 34.

Fines: Sleaford family name.
Pennestone: Huntercombes' family name.
Alford: Tolland's mother.

For a woman to admit that she is in the wrong is so rare as to make her irresistible when she does so.

Enough is as bad as a feast, just as half a loaf is far worse than no bread. St John Clarke.

Mrs Erdleigh is consulted by Katherine, Lady Warminster.

Seduction is to do and say the most banal thing in the most banal way.

Perhaps the last will not be the first in heaven, the first will.

A young hostess who always talks as if she was opening a bazaar.

After all, what is pleasure compared with money.

People who pretend that there is no such thing as being in love or being a gentleman, but all the same retain uneasy doubts.

People who hate and fear the past.

Training a wife or mistress like the training of the Spanish Riding School.

The difference between people who want to excel, and those who just want to do a thing frightfully well.

Goodhart's story of the dervish fighting his way into the British square . . . something appealing to a schoolmaster in the notion of someone being able to read in the midst of appalling tumult. (?as dialogue).

'How are you?' 'Well, I seem to have neutralized the death wish for the moment.'

An officer like Mime in *Siegfried*, perhaps cleaning a Sam Browne belt.

Pansy son of a Labour peer.

People who find everything significant are almost as boring as people who find nothing significant.

Sir Magnus Donners.

'He had a tidy bit of sickness.'

The appalling thing about the Victorians was not their seriousness but their frivolity – the belief that going deep was easy.

Could you be a saint and mind your own business?

A hostess watches her guests with the air of a croupier at the roulette table, raking in bad conversational counters, putting on bids for more hopeful talking.

Paper Wine (book title).

People who drop their voices at the end of a sentence to give emphasis.

'Just a song at twilight.'

'Stendhal said that he would rather his wife tried to stab him once a week than greeted him every day with a sour face.' 'Mine does both.' 'A little temperament is always nice.'

A pretty Wednesday side.

No doubt it was Tamberlaine's bad leg that made him such a nuisance to the world.

A complexion like a Gruyère cheese.

Poets as a class are so hard on whisky.

One of the most difficult things to realize when one is young is that all the awful odds and ends taking place round one are, in fact, the process of living.

An elderly lady who makes one feel that everything one does or says is very coarse-grained.

'Can't stand these high stools, they make my legs go to sleep.'

Names
Cubitt
Morland or Moreland

Mrs Andriadis had two interests, the ballet and the Spanish Civil War.

X made a face as if showing round a stubbly section of his chin.

'Heather, Heather, she is under the weather.'
'Nearly stopped her there.'

À propos Moreland, artists are in some ways simple people.

If you don't like anyone then a voice on the telephone at once makes it clear.

There are people who like coarse things, and know they like coarse things, but there are also people who like coarse things, but prefer to think they like un-coarse things.

Possibly open while with the Army at Haverford-west.

'It's silly to keep on moaning about it.' 'Well, if he's rough I feel sorry for her.' Overheard.

Womanizing, like alcoholism.

Women will infinitely sacrifice what they want a lot in order to get what they want more, that is usually par for the course.

All the people who complained about the French putting black troops on the Rhine, now complain about the colour bar. All the liberals who were pro-Boer are now anti-apartheid.

The incredible joy it is to have met Umfraville as RTO when travelling.

A doctor, a family doctor, who knows and talks of Erridge. A doctor who knows Moreland.

The Army book should begin with something fairly grim like a suicide.

The people – Bloomsbury etc. – amongst whom one feels the creative instinct dry up.

In one sense *Ulysses* is a much better story than *The Rosary* or *Uncle Tom's Cabin.*

Extreme scepticism is the only possible terms to accept religion. Anything like dogma immediately suggesting unbelief.

'All right, all right, keep your whip up.'

The gentle lowing of a distant air-raid warning.

'After thirty one begins to feel less fit for soldiering.' (Napoleon Bonaparte)

The extraordinary thing of how when a woman looks at her least attractive you sometimes feel her most desirable.

Exhibitionism in love almost a *sine qua non.*

'She's the sort of girl you have never caught out in a floral dress, she would always be in a check,' some woman says.

Very bright, rather apologetic look, that accountants have who deal with money.

'The only thing in life is the knowledge that there is no key to life.'

'Gaze not on swans.'

Self applauding.

The way in which, in England, all intellectual conversation tends to be a kind of weapon in the hands of the speaker.

Without any great physical attractions she had that instinctive gift of making a man feel pleased with himself after talking with her. (?Rosie Manasch.)

'It has been pointed out a thousand times that the awful thing about life is not that you don't get what you want, but that you do.'

A man was playing 'Softly Awakes My Heart' by Saint-Saëns, on an accordion.

The Minister clearly had the idea that everything was easy if one knew the facts.

Names
Goodchild
Joddrill

I have no objection to everyone being equal, but I should like to be equal in the way that smart society is equal, where you can say what you like pretty well, as long as you pull no punches. That is the only genuine equality.

Marriage, the moment when a real step is taken.

The upper classes, with all their faults, are actually the only integrated society. In this respect it would be better if the whole world could be turned into a vast aristocratic world, i.e. interested in each other.

Jenkins meets Le Bas years later. Le Bas says, 'Are you the Jenkins who . . . or the Jenkins who . . . I can remember your face,' etc. Jenkins can only think of Widmerpool to recall himself to Le Bas.

The Army. 'Do you remember that fair boy Williams, T., who went out with the last draft. Well he has copped it.'

After the Jenkins' marriage Lady Molly and Jeavons become their distant relations. A description of the settling down.

Jeavons in later life looking at TV. ?Molly dead. ?with Norman Chandler.

Curved is the line of beauty, straight is the line of duty.

The business of offending someone by doing something completely justifiable, e.g. by being reasonably successful yourself.

The rather punch-drunk air of certain very rich men. (Sir M. Donners.)

A prim, rather silly expression of countenance.

One of the reasons certain people are miserable is because they have read somewhere that happiness consists in working for others.

The idiom of the average modern novel is just as artificial as the writing of the eighteenth century.

Intermediate beings like Satyrs.

Soldiers must be judged to a large extent not by intelligence, but by their will to power.

A literary comparison between Vautrin and Magwitch (been done).

Cousins à la mode de Bretagne.

Moreland remarks, 'Everyone now says that pictures are just a matter of colour and design, and in the same breath praise Picasso, some of whose pictures have as much literary content as *The Last Day in the Old Home* or *Floreat Etona.*'

It is very rare for people who are 'good at their job' to be good at anything else.

It's the very essence of human nature to want everything both ways.

One of the maddest things is to suppose that people could be 'different'.

Adjutant and his assistant, like Tweedledum and Tweedledee.

It was impossible to exaggerate the atmosphere of pure egotism in F Mess.

The banker poets:
Guillaume Apollinaire, T. S. Eliot and Robert W. Service, and James Joyce too.

Here was I with a platoon, but the power had come too late, thirty men were only a bore, a responsibility.

Widmerpool the Rastignac or Rubempré of our day.

?When Stringham gets killed Mrs Foxe lives in a cottage with Norman Chandler, and gets up at six to cook his breakfast etc. Leaves him what is left of her money.

?Erridge. ?Gypsy Jones. Against the war at start, in favour when Russia comes in, later anti-atom plant.

Names
Amy
Orchard
Stacey

'There's been nothing like it since the mutilation of the Herms.'

'It won't be for nothing that Petrarch's Laura was a member of the de Sade family.'

Mark Members, much later, has an affair with ?Lady Huntercombe.

Name
Salvage

It is madness to expect anything of anyone. The sooner you expect anything of anyone life becomes a wilderness of disappointment.

Umfraville running the VIP place at Brussels.

Dai and Shoni took two girls up in a balloon.
The balloon began to lose air.
'What about the women?'
'Oh, fuck the women.'
'But have we time?'

'The hell of a long way after Kafka.'

Some people's selfishness is more agreeable than the abdication of others.

There is a very strange smell here, rather like coarse tobacco.

Life is inevitably empty to power maniacs, that is why so many of the saints seem to have found it so repellent.

'You have women for whom you don't even feel a faint affection, much less love.'

People usually do what they want.

One of the difficulties about writing a novel is that in real life a million small things bring about some situation, which has usually to be represented as the result of one big thing in a book.

The different levels of sexual sophistication in women, but equally their universal instinct for a sexual situation.

Names
Baldwin Hodges

Statues under the Ground

Jean marries a Spaniard.

American: Madame Brilliantine. She wears spectacles, possibly sun spectacles.

?Frederica ends up as a lesbian with Heather Hopkins.

The peculiar relationships of the *amitié amoureuse.* (Rosie Manasch)

The consolations of a religion in which someone does not believe.

One of St John Clarke's books, *E'en the Longest River.*

Looking as if he were perpetually facing life's court-martial.

Mood music.

A kind of retreat from perfectionism.

Music for a dentist's waiting-room.

Chandler, like Jeavons, develops an upper-class manner, later both grey-haired and distinguished.

Sir Magnus Donners falls in love with a tart. Barnby finds himself employing the same tart.

Somebody edits the life and letters of St John Clarke.

Being trivial is not doing the washing up, so much as minding doing the washing up.

The Military Philosophers.

People wanting a higher rank in the Army, and putting everything into it, like competing with people in love.

The real test of a man is the sort of woman he wants to marry.

The nearest some women get to being faithful to their husbands is being disagreeable to their lovers.

Tunes: 'I'm Forever Blowing Bubbles', 'If I Should Plant a Tiny Seed of Love in your Heart', 'Back Home in Tennessee'.

A woman who memorises phrases from reviews, and brings them out in conversation.

'Like good morals, one likes some people to have them, even though one may not want them oneself.'

Mrs Foxe had married Buster about 1920.

The Benediction of the Swords (Meyerbeer's *Les Huguenots*). *Blessing the Swords. Benediction of Swords.*

Supex's office = Ruffman. 'Women who can't spell ought to be thrashed.'

Clasen, as Prince Theodoric's, ADC.

'His mentor proved a devotee of Bacchus,'

Possibly in the end Erridge marries Gypsy Jones. Both moderate members of the Labour Party only, 1940 or later.

The extraordinary thing about the war was that people who really didn't want to be involved in it were not involved in it, comparatively speaking.

Days of Abdication
Casanova's Chinese Restaurant (Book titles)

If you ask people about their job, very few have any idea of its general implications.

The Fetichists (novel title?)

'If there is a hell, and I suppose if there is one, I will probably go to it.'

Many successful men cannot take the final plunge of entry into the upper classes, as much from choice as anything else.

Humbug consists in making claims to a degree of moral or intellectual purity, or disinterestedness, that you do not possess or seriously try to attain.

?Anne Stepney eventually marries Quiggin.

Jeavons hums:
'For her hero was a pierrot.
A pierrot on the Portobello Pier.'

Moreland says that Matilda ceased to love him after they had been married for a time. Jenkins says that she said she did love Moreland at Mrs Foxe's party. Reflection on general mess of such things.

The intimacy of English life makes for snobbery, if you like to call it that.

A possible *partie carrée* in a later volume, Erridge and Gypsy Jones, now husband and wife, entertaining Quiggin and Lady Anne Quiggin, née Stepney.

Writers, especially novelists, have a lot to express which they cannot put down in their own person.

The awful boredom of living among men only (the Army).

You can only control the situation if you are not really in love.

Dividend vouchers going back to the South Sea Bubble.

No lesson is more difficult for a young man to learn than the fact that, because a woman loves him, does not mean she wants to do as he wants.

One of the strange things about the Victorians was seeing refinement in women, whereas one of the attractions of women is their extreme coarseness.

Fear has much in common with jealousy in the sudden violent, unexpected realization that you are not loved by someone you adore. (cf. air raids and bad manners.)

Madame a plaisir.

Maclintick used to be very much against Jesus, but I always found him a God one can't help liking, even though someone reminded me he didn't do any of the difficult things, like marrying and having children.

Lord Huntercombe's Benozzo Gozzoli had been identified by Berenson himself.

She had that touch of monstrosity that can be attractive.

Was Herodias in love with her husband?

The disgusting feeling when a woman suddenly ceases to love you.

Basta!

It's going to be age at the prow, and pain at the helm, as the elderly sadist said (?Moreland).

X went out of the company office, bringing what for me was one of those rare and delicious moments in the Army when one was left alone.

One of the awful things about life is not how 'nasty' people are, but how nasty 'nice' people can be.

There is no substitute for suffering.

Far easier to choose relations than friends.

The remembered moaning in pleasure of someone loved, haunting the memory.

If you are thwarted in love you can sometimes, as it were, shift the whole emotion bodily, if only in a superficial way, on to another person, the psychology of the rebound, cf. kissing Madame D instead of Suzette.

If you enjoy certain things, you must accept certain other things.

'The characteristic women most detest in man is unselfishness,' said X. 'They don't often have to worry, but how their wives must have hated those saintly kings in the Middle Ages.'

Sacred and Profane Love, the excellence of the classic conception.

'And all my days are trances,
And all my nightly dreams
Are where thy grey eye glances,
And where thy footstep gleams–
In what ethereal dances
By what eternal streams.'
(Edgar Allan Poe, 'To One in Paradise')

'Then with strange adultery
Dost in each heart a brothel keep
Awake all men do lust for thee
And some enjoy thee when they sleep.'
(Rochester)

Lust gives that grim, pounding feeling, like heavy guns in the distance.

'I am the most modest man in the world,' said Moreland. 'When it is a question of women falling in love with me, I never expect it, but when it has happened I can never believe that they will not suddenly fall in love with someone else.'

A point left out in romantic historical novels, that the hero marries the girl, but the hero worries that the girl may fall in love with a man who kidnaps her, e.g. *I Promessi Sposi.*

In good society you are always meeting people of more importance than yourself. Some individuals – even those naturally born to this society – can never stand that.

The business of loving people for all sorts of unexpected reasons, sometimes things which they themselves think disadvantageous.

When the 'Modern Movement in art' came in, did a different sort of person seize 'power', or were they the same people as the old artists and critics?

When you begin to examine what people are like you get involved into the past – with relations you know too much.

Some people think anything can be expressed in words, but words are so coarse a medium that some things can only be felt.

'How terribly unamusing, unoriginal are the minds of women,' says X after some disappointment in love.

'Like the lame girl in Dostoevsky who didn't want to be happy.'

Although 'artists' may, in practice, be very egotistical, they are at least, in theory, more interested in other people than the rest of the world, certainly more interested than politicians.

The Mute with the Bow String. (*?Arabian Nights.*)

Stringham, a private in the RAOC, meeting at Wheeler's.
'The fact is one is not a great deal of use as a mess waiter.'

As constipated as an owl.

One has often been told by colonial administrators that if you are nice to black people they think you are weak. A lot of white people are like that too, especially female ones.

Names
Fritcher
Soper

Love, like a fearful din in your ears.

Jenkins indescribably glad to see Widmerpool when they meet in the Army?

Some people propose, as a form of going 'one better', the final compliment they cannot resist.

'Don't be a prisoner of the old dogmas.'

Someone's wife leaves him, and he complains that the situation is usually reported as people moving apart, but on the contrary he thought they were getting on splendidly.

You can't make the classless society retroactive.

It was one of those books written to make people feel that it is all rather fun to get old and die.

'With all royalties, knights' fees, advowsons, privileges, liberties, customs, awards, marriages, reliefs, escheats, forfeitures, chases, parks, warriors, etc.'

Roland Gwatkin, keen territorial company commander falls in love, neglects his duties. He is cut out by some spurious civilian, sent to a holding battalion.

'Arm in arm together
Just like we used to be
Stepping out along with you
Meant all the world to me.'
⎫
⎬ Welsh troops singing
⎭

England is a country where everything depends on knowing the right people without defining who the right people may be. Very possibly not the apparently obvious ones.

Everything depends on the special rather than the general, the 'right' people are not necessarily the grandest people.

Love is always a question of Nature abhorring a vacuum, at least where a woman is concerned. She looks about and then falls.

The men who advocate women being educated only to the domestic virtues rarely run after that sort of women for themselves.

Match Me Such Marvel

People are boring, but not *life*.

The English love buffoons.

Women's liking for a man who does not take love too seriously.

One so often reads that the world of 'good society' is an 'empty one', but is it any emptier than any other society?

'There's a long, long trail a-winding
Into the land of my dreams,
Where the nightingales are singing
And a white moon beams.
There's a long, long night of waiting
Till my dreams all come true . . . '

The quality that women lack is magnanimity.

People who take on 'behaving well' in life are landed with that position for good. Any deviation is regarded by the world as much worse than those who make a habit of 'behaving badly'.

The way in which certain literary critics by abusing a book or play, make you sure you will like it.

Both sexes: feeling of gratitude after making love to someone successfully, which results in being able to put up with a lot from them.

People's extraordinary certainty about what will happen after a professional or social change is made, e.g. the class system abolished.

The moment in the war when about 1,600, including regular officers, were sacked, when another, similar, man simply took their place.

Love is like being seasick, you feel you are going to die, then when you walk down the gangway on to dry land you can hardly remember what you have suffered.

There is always a yearning in England for strong-willed buffoons, even intellectual ones will serve.

Articles: 'Spring comes to the West'. 'Sunset on Armistice Day'.

Ability – being brought a mass of papers and knowing how to deal with them.

Tokenhouse (*Name*)

'Falling out of love is almost as enjoyable as falling in love,' said X. ?Priscilla (said by Pam Berry).

The actual existence of other people gets on the nerves of some individuals.

'His stories have the abstract quality of pure extentionism.'

Supposing one were Louis XV or someone like that, it would be just as 'bad'.

All love affairs are special cases, and yet at the same time each is the same case.

The art of war is the choice of men.

Widmerpool's mother dies in circumstances in which he has not gone to see her for some snobbish or communist reason.

When Matilda is a hostess, she shows Jenkins the photographs of the Seven Deadly Sins.

Literary critics as a class are conceited, irresponsible, badly informed and not deeply interested in the technique of writing. ?says Quiggin.

People are unfaithful when they feel they are at the crest of the wave.

Men less naturally promiscuous than women?

Is imagination the friend or enemy of love?

Nothing irritates people more than self-control.

Guggenbühl changes his name, and becomes a successful TV don.

?When Jean reappears, she tells Jenkins about an unhappy love affair.

The incompetence of solicitors makes even publishers seem efficient.

Did Templer ever get off with Anne?

Life would be all right, if you could say it was always people's own fault, or alternatively if it was all fate. As it is both work unfairly.

There is nothing more undignified than being in the wrong, and not admitting it.

Moral self-indulgence, just the same as physical self-indulgence in its results.

The relationship of officer and servant.

Widmerpool possibly mixed up in a 'secrets case'.

Friendship, like love, carries the seeds of disillusion in it.

Stringham dies in a Japanese POW camp.

?Gwatkin is killed in some unromantic way.

Bogbourne (*Place*).

'Like Paris, whom he somewhat resembled, he preferred Aphrodite to Hera or Athene.'

The doubtful truth of the English taking their pleasures sadly – yelling, buffoonery etc.

'No action with illusion, nature.'

Funeral Games

The happiness of the Home Guard.

Moreland, when he marries Mrs Maclintick, tells Jenkins that at least she goes some way to appreciating him as an artist.

Santos (*Name*).

'For some are sick, and some are sad,
And some have never loved Thee well,
And some have lost the love they had.'
(Henry Twells, 'At Even, when the Sun did Set')

'I told him idealization of working-class life is only a form of repressed homosexuality.'

Iron Age Kings (Book title)

Some apparently desk-bound officer is killed in a plane on the way to America.

Someone pees on Widmerpool and Fettiplace-Jones, during an Army exercise. ?Sunny Farebrother.

Fettiplace-Jones is a full colonel and welfare officer, to whom Widmerpool is sucking up.

One of the most difficult conceptions for stupid people to grasp is that you can be fed up with life, not displeased with certain social or political conditions, but fed up with the whole affair.

Dicky Umfraville has his revenge on Buster in a later volume. Does it in alliance with Miss Weedon ?via General Conyers.

Heightened bisexuality.

"Hear you are a writer, I always read *Blackwood's*, amazing how they keep up the standard."

The hero of yesterday is the *maquereau* of tomorrow.

After the war, Sir Magnus does needlework.

Once you have declared your love the whole situation changes, like the recruiting sergeant's manner on getting you to take the shilling, and then seeing you in the barracks.

The fact of their being dynamic – part of action – is the thing that makes many painful experiences possible to bear.

You learn in due course that certain physical types are more or less emotionally subject to you.

Few reviewers try to find out what an author thinks, they are only interested in praising or picking holes to show their own qualities.

'Comme le souvenir est voisin du remords.'
(Victor Hugo)

Jenkins possibly meets Gwatkin later, cf. old captain in Lermontov in reverse.

Return to Cunneda at the end of the war trilogy.

Stripling in old age, collecting vintage cars, last seen wearing a deerstalker and Inverness cape, driving one, very happy.

Odo Stevens and Quiggin become great friends after the war.

Sad Captains } (Book titles)
Sad Majors   }

'How many battles have you been in?' 'Endless, I've a VC and two bars but I don't wear the ribbon, out of modesty.'

The whole series ends with Jenkins looking out of a window at the men working in the street from a room in which some incident has been taking place, possibly Widmerpool walking away, as he walked in out of the fog.

A wound that passes unperceived, but which annihilates, like Chinese executioner severing a head without removing it from the body.

Purged Not in Lethe. (Book title)

'I sent my love back to the lovely time.' (Swinburne)

Jenkins, by then a major, meets Kedward in Belgium, who salutes him and calls him 'Sir'.

Odo Stevens' war contrasted with Stringham's. ?Stevens kept after the war by Stringham's sister Flavia?

'One doesn't really get into the big money until one's a Major.' (Hubert Duggan)

'The older one gets the more one can't stand it all a moment longer, yet the less one wants to die.' ?Moreland.

Names
Tuttle
Tidy

The position required a certain bogusness in the arts, anyway to be found in nearly all the great practitioners of them.

Nightmares of boredom and melancholy oozed from him.

'Is George still joint-Master?'

He was run over by a victoria in Assouan.

The ritual killing of the King after seven or nine years, like the death of love in which the woman kills the man.

Horus, God of the morning sun, Anubis the jackal, Horus the falcon.

'Scenes of licence which would have scandalized the Court of Caligula.'

'We'll do it with grace' (Egyptian workmen singing).

People are attracted by treachery.

'Camel ride to the tomb.'

Mansions of Mars. (Book title)

'Good morning, Sergeant Major, here's a sparra for your cat.'

The Pharaoh in whose reign a sheep spoke.

'Nought but profounder hell can be his shroud' (Milton on *Osiris*) (Mr Deacon).

Passionless.

Robbins. Unpleasant PM, course commandant (died 1981).

Soper's sophistication about food, albeit Army food, impressed Biggs, however unwillingly.

'One of the things about having too many women is that it turns a man into a woman.'

The vortex of becoming.
The abode of asymmetry.

The difference between doing a thing, and saying you are doing it, e.g. writers of frank confessions who to some extent *develop* the act by admitting to it.

A book of poems: *Secretions.*

The unknown mourner who strewed flowers on Nero's tomb.

English geisha.

?Japanese (?oriental) women: submission, yet at ease with men.

Moreland says, 'I hope there'll be a lot of laughter at my funeral.'

Everything might be all right, but somehow it isn't.

Members and Quiggin grumble about each other's war record.

The English, unlike the Americans or even continentals, never really believe in the existence of the world around them.

Young married woman, with lots of children, having affairs, laying down the law about behaviour, etc.

Certain things are altered by talking about them, like cooling boiling water when you put a spoon in.

Dempster. (*Name*)

It is always assumed that everyone has all the qualities of a human being; in fact not many individuals have more than a few of them.

?Use Sir Magnus Donners as Desmond Morton (in going to PM to arrange for immediate transference of Belgian Resistance to GB).

Ingoldsby Legends: account of St Paul's Victory Service.

Nothing is ever settled.

V1's shuddering.

'A critic so despicable one would not mind, even if he liked one's work.' ?Moreland says.

'To me it's taking you out, to you it's being taken out by me.'

Balance of Payments. (Title)

Just as certain things cannot be put on the stage, actors are not sufficiently subtle to express them, certain things cannot be achieved in life, human beings are not subtle enough to achieve them.

It's not what happens to people that matters, but what they think happens to them.

Stopped at a Chemist. (?Banned play.)

When Jean returns to London married to a Latin-American Military Attaché she is perhaps seen in the same position in the Ritz as when Jenkins met Quiggin, surrounded by the children of the Ambassador.

'That was in the days when donkeys wore hats.'

A committee to award a literary prize?

Begin war vols with lying in bed in the morning, listening to the V1s coming over.

Nothing is interesting unless you are interested, and conversely.

'A hundred disagreeable sexual experiences.' (Proposed book by Moreland?)

Miscellaneous Equities.

A baby that looks exactly like the father carrying it.

Begin vol. 9 with Polish evacuation. 'Then one day a telegram came through saying . . .'

Names
Victor
Upjohn
Bowman
Crowder
Wheeler

'With veiled women what you lose on the swings you gain enormously on the roundabouts.'

A hunchback boy was kicking a tin along the road with great gusto.

It is always a mistake to assume that other people have lower standards than oneself.

People who lack address are not necessarily stupid.

'You'll have to play it by ear.'

'The Exterminator will service you on Tuesday.'

Profiles in String

Courthouse Cobb, American Colonel, says 'The US Navy are prohibited alcohol. We should call in their golf clubs I guess.'

Sweet Skin

Life's all right, in a sense, until the bourgeois necessities obtrude themselves, sooner, or later unavoidable.

Iced Water
Vests and Transvests } novels

'Of what avail is power, if not for our satisfaction.'
(Eliphas Levi)

'They are casting lots for my raiment at this very
moment,' someone remarks.

Men who talked or slept with her were often found
frozen to death.

Sending out several million volts of synthetic charm.

Polish name
Kliszczewski

'After all, Sophocles hadn't much humour . . . '

To be something is subtly affected by being adver-
tised as something, e.g. a happily married couple
become somehow different by being photographed
for the papers as a happily married couple.

'The odd feeling of relief sometimes when someone
you love, or you are in love with, puts off a meeting.'

People say to a writer, 'If I could write like you I would,' etc., etc. outlining as a rule some banal moral issue. The point is that a writer writes about what *he* is. If he thought their banal thoughts he would not be a writer.

A great many people make a lot of fuss about what others take completely in their stride.

Vavassor. Porter at the War Office.

As one gets older life gets more and more like the ghost story of the man walking over the break-waters, seeing something following him, and for some reason breaking into a run.

'Part of the time one feels one would rather like to die, and the rest of the time one does not want to die at all but is about to.' (?Moreland)

People with strong personalities often have weak characters.

'If love is *enfant de bohème*, masochism is the stepbrother of hypochondria.'

'Walking down the Strand
Met in Piccadilly
Clapstruck Susie Ann
And Syphilitic Billy.' (Old song)

Restaurant: The Impenitent Bachelor.

People who want all the fun of pontificating about the arts without any of the trouble.

A cat muezzin calling other cats to prayer.

Cambises. 'A lamentable tragedy full of pleasant mirth.'

Names
Pontner
Kotecke
Schoenmakers
Gondobert
Gondomir
Wisznierski
Szthowscki
Theodomir
Bohemond
Zaiezkowski
Terzeciak
Jezierski

'Visiting her was like calling on Penelope when the suitors were about the house.'

Quite a considerable part of being intelligent consists in an ability to listen to what other people say.

A man who likes photography, 'Angry Seas', etc.

Pipe bore, blows one ring through another while watching TV.

The extraordinary stupidity and conceit of human beings is being unable to understand that someone who reveals themself in a diary, e.g. Pepys or Boswell, is not inferior to themselves, but greatly superior.

In the end, the best one hopes for is explaining a few things to oneself.

It is difficult to think of anything worse happening to people one dislikes, than what actually does happen to them.

Gauguin abandoned business for the arts, Rimbaud the arts for business.

A fortune-teller, who can only tell you something extraneous to what you want to know, has something of the novelist's (true) powers.

There is perhaps a question, at the end of the book, about putting up a stained-glass window to Erridge in the church.

A play about a man who is in love with his father?

The politician, like the artist, has far from total control over what he does, i.e. it is not 'logical', which explains some of the extraordinary things politicians do.

Bugs to buggery in three generations.

Life is an examination, in which there are questions but no answers.

Winter's Traces
Mute of Malice } Book titles

Self-control is so rare as to be very little understood.

After the War
Births and Deaths } Book titles
Slow on the Feather

'Nobody enjoys a Jocasta more than I do.'

Trapnel shouts, 'Fossil of dung — coprolite — faecal débris — petrified shit — sodomitical monkey.'

It is a great object for critics to prove not that books are very important but that criticism is very important.

The Winter Solstice.

One of the things one did not expect when younger was that friends quite simply dislike one being even relatively successful. Something that could earlier have been learned from reading biographies.

Last Days of Carnival.

The disagreeable aspect of so many people is not so much their doing unpleasant things, as wanting to justify them.

Into the Mist
Bin Ends   } (book titles)
Golden Grind

Widmerpool says at the end, 'I have had a happy life on the whole, I think I can say people have liked me etc.'

The Autumn Solstice.

$$\left.\begin{array}{l} \text{Latroon} \\ \text{Krasda} \\ \text{Jordan} \\ \text{Lebanon} \end{array}\right\} \text{wines}$$

Widmerpool at the end of the books says, 'I have had an interesting life, and a not entirely unsuccessful one.'

The Burton quotation ('I hear new news every day . . .') also at the end.

In the distance the pounding of the centaurs' hooves died away, the flames of their torches no longer lit up the frozen sea.

Books Do Furnish a Room (Book title)

'We know Pilate washed his hands,' said X, 'the point is, did he wash his feet?'

Cat chasing birds from snow.

A film of Musil's *Man Without Qualities,* directed by Stroheim.

Masochism is only sadism towards yourself. In the same way anti-authority is only another angle from which to exercise authority.

People who like to tell other people how to behave.

The rather fatuous facial expression of some Indian holy men.

One touch of Nietzsche makes the whole world kin.

The past tends to worry men more than women.

Anguish and Recompense.

The expanding as well as the contracting of life, as one grows older.

There have never been any real salons in England, because everyone here thinks a salon is a place for a free meal rather than for conversation.

There is an element of the businessman in all Americans, especially the literary critics.

Someone has Pamela Flitton after she is dead, though unaware that this has happened. ?Widmerpool, Craggs.

A wine snob boasts that he has some bottles corked with corks made from Proust's soundproof room.

Clown. Compare? 'I'll tell you all the devil's names he calls upon are but fustian names, gathered out of Welsh heraldry.'
(Beaumont and Fletcher, *The Fair Maid of the Inn*, Act IV)

Growing old feels like being increasingly penalized for a crime you haven't committed.

Trapnel's books are republished in the last volume of *The Music of Time*.

That curiously masculine look that women who have been had by a great many men get in later life. Women of this sort tend to two types, those who immediately draw you into themselves with a kiss and a squeeze, those who present an unfriendly façade and rough manner.

In one's sixties, 'You will soon be sixty-five,' etc., one begins to feel, 'Well it's been very kind to allow me to stay so long etc.'

Dogs have no uncles nor Kings relations. (Indian proverb)

The third concoction (Burton, blood, etc.) (in *Books*).

The Bitch Pack Hunts on Wednesday (?Title of a book).

Maliphant (Name)

Excuse the Cliché (Title of a novel).

A man totally without the quality of loyalty.

The Electric Blanket, a nightclub.

Shackerly. A writer?

Does Anne Stepney finally organize student riots?

'Writes about Rilke as if he were an Austrian Rupert Brooke.' (A critic)

Nuns and actresses the same. Gérard de Nerval.
(Matilda? Polly?)

Temporary kings (Frazer).

'The dark is my delight,
So 'tis the nightingale's.
My music's in the night,
So is the nightingale's.
My body is but little,
So is the nightingale's.
I love to sleep 'gainst prickle,
So doth the nightingale.'
Song from John Marston's *The Dutch Courtesan*, Act
1, Scene 2

To keep the ball rolling, I asked Marlow if this
Powell was remarkable in any way. 'He was not
exactly remarkable,' Marlow answered, with his
usual nonchalance, 'in a general way it's very
difficult for one to become remarkable, people won't
take sufficient notice of one, don't you know.'
(Conrad, *Chance.*)

Wilt thou upon the high and giddy mast send up the
ship's boy's eyes and risk his brains – a TV mast.

'This is beyond melancholy'
(Webster, *The White Devil*)

In So Many Words (memoirs).

The Persepolis, or Persepolitan, outline of
Battersea Power Station.

Adonis was grandson of Pygmalion, but not by the
statue.

A playboy priest.

Love affair while going bathing, taking clothes off.

'It's because we are using the burning cost basis'
(insurance).

The Last Judgement ⎫
The Triumph of Death ⎬ (Book titles)

Christ in the House of Lévi-Strauss? (a picture).

The appalling difficulties of writing well become
clear only as one gets older.

How to write a good Jewish novel – write a good novel, and give the characters Jewish names.

Woman's name:
Fleur de Lys (Glober's wife, one of them).

Brothel in the Bario Chino, Barcelona.

All things visible and televisible – the television of the body and of the life everlasting.

How difficult to know when writing about them, for instance, where the emphasis of any given individual's life weighs most heavily.

In all ages there is a great battle against intelligence, against the arts, but the attack takes different forms in different epochs.

The important secrets in war are apt to boil down to such information, as to how many lorries are out of commission, shortages of oil, or how many married men over forty are relatively fit.

In the 1970s, extraordinary pictures imagined of the 1920s and 30s.

'I am the Queen of Samothrace
God, making roses, made my face
In Shushan towards Ecbatain
I wrought my joys with tears and pain.'
(Swinburne, *Queens*)

Offa's Dyke, a study in Anglo-Saxon lesbianism.

'The Swiss' only invention, the cuckoo clock,' comes
from Whistler's 'Ten o'clock Lectures, p. 156, *The
Gentle Art of Making Enemies*, 1885.

'He doesn't know Maxim Wledig from Maxim
Gorki.' ?Dr Brightman.

The last vol: ?Widmerpool dead, a book written
about him?

The last vol. Mr Deacon's paintings are being
'collected', perhaps Hugo Tolland involved in this.

The popular confusion of compassion with self-pity.

St John Clarke has to wait for TV to be filmed in the
last volume. ?Or not?

In a sense one knows more about the personalities of Balzac and Dickens from their novels, than of Rousseau and Casanova from their confessions.

'He's in the crude?'
'Crude oil.'
'Exports it from Canada.'

Does Stourwater become an institution, possibly a school, where a child in the book goes at the end?

Things that are known are not necessarily better said.

A play about Oedipus beginning with Oedipus visiting his oculist. 'Can hardly see at all, etc. It followed a road accident.'

Quantitative equivalents.

A novel is simply one means of giving information.

Critics give themselves away, not by what they don't like, but by what they do.

Reading novels demands almost as much talent as writing them.

It is always difficult for a man to grasp that a woman can be passionately in love with him, without making the smallest effort to please him.

Dr Trelawney becomes a hippy cult figure, just as St John Clarke's novels are made into successful films, and Mr Deacon is given a show as a symbolist.

An allegorical picture, Deceit, Friendship, Age and Strife. ?Bronzino.

The embarrassing but valid prerequisite of 'If'.

You start off by thinking of friendships as something devoted, but in the end you are lucky if a friend remembers some quite trivial matter that concerns you, which in fact isn't actually undermining you.

'A mitigated cowboy' (James).

Uninteresting Experience (title for an autobiography).

Narrator writing an autobiography in the last vol.

'The face was all that now remained of thee
No more woman, yet nor quite a tree.'
(Pope, *Dryope*)

'Hayseed, hence.' (*The Tempest*)

'The canker galls the infants of the spring.' (*Hamlet*,
Act V, Scene 1)

Infants of the Spring (Book title).

Cain's jaw-bone (*Hamlet*, Act V, Scene 1).

An essential of any serious work of art is that an
effort has to be made at the receiving end.

'For some we love the loveliest and the best
That from his vintage rolling time hath pressed.'

The Turn of the Days

'Kind hearts are more than coronets
And simple faith than Mormon blood.'

O! Rare Chips Channon.

A man who looked as if he had been pressed for a long time between the pages of a book.

'She's a most triumphant lady, if reports be square for her.' (*Antony and Cleopatra*, II,2)

'How's that for exposure?'

'Here's to the wings of love
May they never lose a feather
'Til your little shoes and my big boots
Stand outside the door together.'

Death in Venice, a Mann's a man for a' that.

The autumn is the great time for fan letters.

Routine incidents, being interviewed for the *Paris Review* and the piece never appearing. Receiving a notification that one has been appointed a Knight of Mark Twain, both happening every few years.

The jealousy of well-placed people for those in touch with them who are less well-placed.

Family Phantoms and other Autobiographical Papers (suggested title).

Compared with whom, Regan and Goneril were devoted daughters.

The narrator is asked to write a memoir of Widmerpool, or interview on TV by someone.

Looking about him, like Stonewall Jackson riding into Frederick.

Tolpuddle Court. A block of flats.

Cause of fatality.

Christ the Capricornian.

As the Cuban defector said to the CIA man, 'You know how it is in Havana in the Early Warning?' (but in the book, 'there in the early morning in Havana.' Hemingway)

It is common to find energy without charm, but charm usually includes energy.

?Widmerpool dies in a hijacked plane.

The Geordies begin at Barnet.

Duport in a wheelchair.

From inventing the wheel, it was only a step to the roulette board.

The Highway of the Dead.

Augustus Egg and Francis Bacon – artists at the breakfast table.

Voluntary suicide as a cure: Aristides.

The coldness of later life.

Roger Chetwode's method with important bankers, of asking a question he had looked up already in a book about banking.

Winter Wait (Doomsday House).

Generally speaking, the intrusion of homosexuals into a world other than their own (rough stuff) is easier than perhaps for heterosexuals. cf. homosexuality as a form of Marxism.

People so rarely believe one when one is speaking the truth.

There are not many advantages in growing old; there are a few. One, that one better appreciates good writers of the past. Two, that one sees the end of a few contemporary stories.

X never forgot a kindness, never failing to be disobliging about anybody who had done him one.

The Aztec ball game. The captain of the winning side executed, and if a goal was scored the teams had all the onlookers' clothes and jewels.

Hearing Secret Harmonies (Thomas Vaughan).

'Should the killer think "I kill or be killed" or "I have been killed", neither is right. He kills not if not killed.' (Hindu Scriptures)

'Lust is a spirit whosoe'er doth raise
The next man that encounters boldly lays.'
(*The Atheist's Tragedy*, Act 2, Scene 3)

Shown as a Loss.

So odious are human beings, that to know all is to pardon nothing.

A demonstration 'that looked like the soldier in Mandalay, who walked with fifty housemaids out of Chelsea to the Strand'. (?Members.)

Names
Todman
Aldredge
Gauntlett
Clement
Dunch
Salter

'Death's head deceived by hold, such is the trust to all mortality.' (*The Atheist's Tragedy*)

'My study's ornament, thou shell of death
Once the bright face of my betrothed lady.'
(*The Revenger's Tragedy*, Act 1, Scene 1)

Delavaquerie
Defresne
Falconer
Dubreucq
Del Cambre

'She was having an affair with two knights, and known as Krak des Chevaliers.'

Sonnets indicating the Young Man was a reviewer: LXXIV, LXXVII, LXXXII.

Hangovers, like summer lightning.

A computer dating.

Cats: Blogram, Vautrain, Lord Jim, Gentleman Brown, Zero.

The sowgelder's song in *Beggar's Bush*, Beaumont and Fletcher, Act 3, Scene 1:

'Take her, and hug her,
And turn her and tug her,
And turn her again boy, again
Then if she mumble,
or if her tail tumble,
Kiss her amain, boy, amain.

It is a rule, almost without exception, that writers and painters, who are always talking about being artists, break down at just that level.

Name
Longbourne

Is there a doctrinaire in the house?

One of the basic human rights is to make fun of people. It is now threatened.

The English have the reputation on the continent of being 'bored'. This is perhaps not so much the ennui of the dandy, as a natural impatience in following through situations.

Other people's despair is merely irritating.

'There mournful *Cypresse* grew in greatest store;
And trees of bitter *Gall*; and *Heben* sad;
Dead sleeping *Poppy*; and black *Hellebore*;
Cold *Coloquintida*; and *Tetra* mad;
Mortall *Samnitis*; and *Cicuta* bad,
With which th'unjust *Athenians* made to dy
Wise *Socrates*, who thereof quaffing glad
Pourd out his life, and last philosophy
To the fayre *Critias*, his dearest belamy.'
(*The Faerie Queene*, 2nd book, VII, 58.

Books on love in the London Library kept under 'Science and Miscellaneous'.

'*Un roman est comme un archet la caisse du violon, qui rend le son c'est l'âme du lecteur.*'
(Stendhal, *Vie de Henri Brulard*)

'The daring pleasure of youth as yet undaunted by any previous fall.' (*Mr Sponge*)

Far Away Friends.

Literary criticism must largely consist of people who can't write, explaining what is wrong with the books of people who can write.

He had taken an aegrotat in the university of life.

'Oh think, how to his latest day,
When Death, just hovering, claim'd his prey,
With Palinure's unalter'd mood,
Firm at his dangerous post he stood,
Each call for needful rest repell'd
With dying hand the rudder held,
Till, in his fall, with faithful sway,
The steerage of the realm gave way.'
(Scott, *Marmion*, Canto 1)

'Dreadful daylight.' (Betjeman)

'In Deheubarth, that now South Wales is hight,
What time King Ryence reign'd and dealed right.'
(*The Faerie Queene*, 3rd book, II, 18)

'From the swift Barry, tombling down apace
Emongst the woody hilles of Dyneuowre;
But dare thou not, I charge, in any case
To enter into that same balefull bowre.'
(*The Faerie Queene*, 3rd book, III, 8)

Unenviable Reputations (?title)

'I'll meet you in the valleys.' (*Cymbeline*)

Cymbals in Naxos.

'Go, bid the soldiers shoot.' (*Hamlet*)

'Which neither spring nor winter's frown
Can ought improve or ought impair.'
(*Strode*)

Beyond the Pleasure Principle

'Glory is like a circle in the waters.'
(*Henry IV, Part* 1, II)

DECIUS: Here lies the east; doth not the day break
here?
CASCA: No.
CINNA: O, pardon, Sir, it doth, and yon grey lines
That fret the clouds, are messengers of day.'
(*Julius Caesar*, II, 1)

Parallels between the equipment kept solely for
Inspections in the Army, and ideas handed out to
interviewers, etc.

'The rough torrent of occasion.'
(*Henry IV Part* 2, IV)

Barrack damages.

'As we are worked with art.'
(*The Winters Tale*, V, 3)

Everyone is at least three people, what they are,
what they think they are, what the world thinks
they are.

'This news has made thee a most ugly man.'
(*King John*, II, 2)

Extraordinary that, after Turner, Impressionism seemed altogether new; and 'modern poetry' after Browning.

Decadence does not consist in the showing up of the corruption of society, but in the concealing of it.

'She's able to freeze the God Priapus and undo a whole generation.'
(*Pericles*, IV, 6)

Writing about small aristocratic societies is condemned as having no general bearing, but after all Oedipus was king of Thebes.

'Horribly stuffed with epithets of war.'
(*Othello*, I, 1)

'Excellent wretch.'
(*Othello*, III, 3)

'Wide and more wide it spreads all the realm
E'en Palinurus nodded at the helm.' (*Dunciad*)

Her Majesty the Queen. Jubilee Ode.
Though she may not ponder Borges
When she's cutting meat for corgis
At least a dozen answer to her helm
And in visiting a NAAFI
She rarely quotes Cavafy
She's an expert on the bloodstock of her realm.
Chorus: She's an expert on the bloodstock of her realm.

'He, after Eve seduc'd, unminded shrunk
Into the wood fast by.'
(Milton, *Paradise Lost*, 10, 332)

Rumours of War

One might vary Tolstoy's comment on happy and unhappy families, by saying that all novelists have the same problem, every autobiographer a different problem.

From *Lucky Alphonse* to *Lucky Jim*.

'Toute la verité n'est pas bonne à dire.'

An inverted Pentheus, held together, rather than torn apart, by the Maenads. (Connolly at *Horizon*)

'Finish, good lady; the bright day is done,
And we are for the dark.'
(*Antony and Cleopatra*, V, 2)

'Anybody can get along on level ground,' said the
old man laconically. 'Not with equal swiftness,' said
I . . . 'nor can I assert that even Powell himself, the
first of all road walkers, was entitled to so bright a
wreath of fame as the Snowdon Ranger.'
(Borrow, *Wild Wales*, Chapter 44 (from John
Saumarez Smith))

Chatterley a name in Surtees. ?Lawrence got it
from there. cf. 'Game Keepers', *Mr Romford's
Hounds*, Chapter 1, page 161.

A sequel to Kim, *His Life in the Secret Service.*

You can't be a creative artist if you are in any
restrictive sense an intellectual snob.

'Scarus, we'll beat them into bench holes. I have yet
Room for six scotches more.'
(*Antony and Cleopatra*, IV, 7)

KENT: 'Sir, 'tis my occupation to be plain,
I have seen better faces in my time
Than stands on any shoulder that I see
Before me at this instant.'
(*King Lear*, II, 2)

NURSE: 'Anon, anon!
Come, let's away; the strangers all are gone.'
(*Romeo and Juliet*, I, 5, line 146)

A thief crucified between two Christs.

A claret, Château Naboth.

'For that which would seem treason in our lives is
laughter when we are dead.'
(*Revenger's Tragedy*, Tourneur)

THE DUCHESS: 'Who ist there dare suspect on this
or these?
May not we deal our favours where we please.'
(*Revenger's Tragedy*, IV, 3)

'Saint-Loup n'était pas assez intelligent pour comprendre que la valeur intellectuelle n'a rien à voir avec une certaine formule esthétique ... ne jugeant chaque chose qu'un poids d'intelligence qu'elle contient, ne perçevant pas les enchantments d'imagination que me donnent certaines qu'il juge frivoles ...' (early appearance of Saint-Loup in Proust).

Of a friend: 'We admired each other innumerable years ago and now we distrust each other with intimate understanding.' (Musil, *The Man Without Qualities*, Book 1, chapter 14)

'And since true love sickness is not desire for possession, but only a gentle unveiling of the world itself, for the sake of which one willingly renounces possession of the beloved.' (Musil, Book 2.1, chapter 32)

Small Mercies

'Abrogate scurrility, Sir Nathaniel, the ventricle of memory.' (Holofernes in *Love's Labour's Lost*, IV, 2)

His/Her infinite lack of variety has not only been withered by time, but staled by custom.

'The Comic as artistic delivery from the Museum of the Absurd.' (Nietzsche, *Birth of Tragedy*)

Points about Shakespeare: that (a) he was a poet, (b) he had an exceptional grasp of individual character, expressed fictionally; two qualities rarely found together.

He was King Arthur at the Court of the Yankees.

'Satire shou'd, like a polish'd Razor keen,
Wound with a Touch that's scarcely felt or seen,
Thine is an Oyster-Knife, that hacks and hews;
The Rage, but not the Talent to Abuse;
And is in Hate, what Love is in the Stews.'
(Lady Mary Wortley Montagu, Verses addressed to the Imitation of the First Satire of the Second Book of Horace (Pope))

Much current journalism seems to partake of the Spaniard's fart in Webster.

The Taming of the Shrew is not, as usually assumed, an attack on women, but a subtle study of two neurotics who turn out to get on with each other.

One of the Medici got Michelangelo to make a snowman for him. (Vasari)

Orwell – the Byron of the century of the common man.

MARIA: 'Aye, but you must confine yourself within the modest limits of order.' (*Twelfth Night*, I, 3)

A male prostitute called Samphire, because he was a 'dreadful trade'.

By no means all men are able to exploit (put to good purpose in any measure) the fact that a woman is in love with them.

'I had read in the great book of experience that, in important schemes, action is the grand requirement, and the rest must be left to fortune.' (Casanova, Vol. 4, 204)

Henry James' inability to invent good proper names, and his country house names particularly inept.

What Proust calls 'the eternal regret of life'. (Vol. 3, 135, Kilmartin edition)

'*Est-il vrai qu'il habite là avec sa poule?*' Asked by a French delegate after being taken to Austen Chamberlain's flat in Carlisle Gardens, Westminster.

'For pleasure and revenge
Have ears more deaf than adders to the voice
of any true decision.' (*Troilus and Cressida*, II, 2)

'Trip the pert fairies.' (*Comus*)

Setting *The Waste Land* to the Londonderry Air.

Was Raffles just a kleptomaniac?

QUEEN: 'More matter, with less art.
POLONIUS: Madam, I swear I use no art at all.'
(*Hamlet*, II, 2)

Topless in Ilium.

'No palms for winning.' (Swinburne, *Ave atque Vale*)

'Like swift drapes.' (*A Midsummer Night's Dream*, III, 2)

Molybdenum Molly

Glencoe: Who wouldn't want to murder their hosts after staying a fortnight?

The voice that breathed o'er Auden
That earliest wedding day.

The Forte et Dure Press.

Hôtel Bougereau et des Artistes.

An American Catholic apologist, known as the Hunchback of Notre Dame.

A short story about Falstaff when he was page to Thomas Mowbray, Duke of Norfolk.
Second part of *Henry IV*, III, 2.

Absence makes the tart grow fonder. Dowson's *Letters*, February 1892.

Those whom the sods love die young.
(Beardsley's *Letters*, collected by Weintraub)

Nom ne figurant pas sur les boîtes aux lettres.

Dracula's dentist.

'The ashram, the ashram, alone is my home.'

Pepys calls the Sensitive plant the Sensible plant.

Names
Scobell
Silent
Sentinels
Tiptoft
Tredworth
Frieda Lutch

In a novel there is always the risk of something unserious being too serious.

Tolstoy writes somewhere that, after a long reflection, he could not think of anyone morally better than himself, certainly no one who tried harder to be good.

Orcadia. Rain borne on light wind that might at any moment turn to a gale, drove persistently across the circle of Standing Stones. Beyond the promontory and the far side of the water rounded green hills lay soft and mysterious. Only thirty or forty stones remained from the original sixty, so scrupulously laid out, cut one from another, supposedly in megalithic yards for religious ritual, astronomical observation, or both, some five thousand years before. In spite of bad weather there is an exhilaration in the northern air, the remnants of a forgotten island kingdom, the very edge of the Roman world, Thule. On a strange confused jumble of criss-cross graffiti, various in date and craftsmanship, had been incised. The largest and best carved of this lettering, even showing an attempt to add script to the capitals, read: G. ISBISTER 1881 (apparently a common local name).

Henchman.

People who make a point of being rude, either as, say, critics or in the Army, are really in the first rank of their vocation, and usually have something to hide, possibly if only thwarted ambition.

Kindred.
Erda (Christian names)

The idea that someone else might know as much, or even more, was extremely foreign to X.

He ought to run a hospital for sick jokes.

Ambrose.

'I wrote him a letter compared with which *De Profundis*, or Kafka's letter to his father, might be regarded as a Collins.'

The Arab's farewell to his dentist. (Medico.)

Within My Date (memoirs).

The eponymous nourishment of the Earl of Sandwich.

MACBETH: 'Thou hast no speculation in these eyes which thou dost glare with.' (*Macbeth*, III, 4)

The last thing she spent her declining years in doing was declining anyone.

Marxism is the opium of the semi-educated.

In his happier days Oedipus had at least been good at guessing riddles.

'He is a man who has warmed both feet at the fire of life – unfortunately they were feet of clay and cracked.'

'Tis hard to say if greater want of skill
Appears in writing or in judging ill.'
(Pope, *Essay on Criticism*)

For he's a jolly good Fellow of All Souls.

An exasperated priest to his superior: either leave our order or order my leave.

Names
Hales
Horsefield
Beales
Sherwin
Aynsworth

A positive Derby of Trojan horses.

Two Jehovah's Witnesses arrive in the middle of a family embarrassment of some kind.

Letters exchanged between an author and female fan lead to a love affair? a murder? a ghost story?

'Her face the book of praises where is read
Nothing but curious pleasures.'
(*Pericles* , I, 1)

Et ego in suburbia vixi.

Certain people prepared to martyrize themselves, but not to exercise discipline on themselves.

OLIVIA: 'If you be not mad be gone,
If you have reason be brief.'
(*Twelfth Night*, I, 5)

An Irishman, one of the Tame Geese. Irishman on the media.

A Reader's Lear (a book)

'Marxism has changed a lot, we don't have the Marxist writers we used.'

AGRIPPA: 'O! rare for Antony.'
(*Antony and Cleopatra*, II, 2)

Real strength of humour in putting a serious point:
e.g. the film *Divorce Italian Style*. The originators
adumbrating a noble peasant, etc., and Aragno
saying No, it should be funny.

CLEOPATRA: 'All strange and terrible events are
welcome,
But comforts we despise.'
(*Antony and Cleopatra*, IV, 13)

Making hay in the sunset.

'You often heirs of fixed destiny.'
(*Merry Wives of Windsor*, V, 5)

Ignobility of mind.

Valéry on Art : To my mind art is a struggle with
what does not exist.

Prolonged confrontation of any art simply deepens
into insolvable problems.

Activities in which the problems are always indefinite. (*Memoirs of Ernest Renan*)

Tax exiles always mourn.

'My geese cry louder than advertisement.'
(*Much Ado About Nothing*, V, 1)

Mrs Coldharbour (name).

Mrs Wiggs of the cannabis patch.

The form people's self-esteem takes is always interesting, for instance, a queer I know when he had picked up guardsmen told me that when it came to haggling about payment they would say: 'But what about *my* honour?' to which he would reply, 'Well, what about my honour?' (?Henchman says).

Did Tiny Tim not die at all, but grew up to join the firm of Scrooge and Marley and become like Tiny Rowland?

Could Henchman be described as a diabolical Tiny Tim?

IMOGEN: 'I see a maid's life is a tedious one.'
(*Cymbeline*, III, 6)

The Merchant Bankers of Venice.

Notoriety has a stormy affair with the present, fame is happily married to the past.

CLOWN: 'To do this is within the compass of man's wit, and therefore I will attempt the doing it.'
(*Othello*, III, 4)

'Mortality and mercy in Vienna.'
(*Measure for Measure*, I, 1)

A rich left-winger who put his trust in Marx and kept his sherry dry.

Those who live more lives than one, more resurrections than one must undergo as well as more deaths.

Twenty million monkeys typing into infinity would type the works of Shakespeare much sooner than twenty million professors of linguistics.

Under a world of whistles, time and steam
Caboose like they go running through
Ohio, Indiana blind baggage to Cheyenne . . . maybe
Kalamazoo. (Hart Crane, 'The River')

Please adjust your fig leaves before leaving.

'The setting sun and music at the close.'
(*Richard II*, II, 1)

'Our business valued, some twelve days hence
our general forces at Bridgenorth shall meet.'
(*Henry IV Part 1*, III, 2 (the construction reverses
object))

A bore, who at worst would explain the meaning of
life.

The musicians sent for at the Boar's Head to
entertain Mistress Tearsheet in *Henry IV Part 2*
were called Sneak's Noise.

'Whose white investments figure innocence.'
(*Henry IV Part 2*, IV, 1)

'The rough torrent of occasion.'
(*Henry IV Part 2*, IV, 1 (perhaps noted earlier))

'Imagined lands and regions of the moon.'
(*Paradise Lost*, 5, 263)

MARGARET: 'Plantagenet doth quit Plantagenet,
Edward for Edward pays a dying debt.' (*Richard III*,
IV.4)
DUCHESS: 'Brief abstract and record of tedious
days.' (*Richard III*, IV.4)
MARGARET: 'If sorrow can admit society
Tell o'er your woes again by viewing mine.'
(*Richard III*)
DUCHESS: 'Bloody thou art, bloody will be thy end.'
(*Richard III*, IV.4)

It's too late now to die young.

'Portions and parcels are of the dreadful Past.'
(Tennyson, 'The Lotus Eaters'.)

'Excellent hymen.' (*The Duchess of Malfi*, II, 5)

'The legitimate end of fiction is the conveyance of
truth.' (Samuel Johnson 'Waller', *Lives of the Poets*)

'And which the harder is I cannot tell,
To hide true love or make false love look well.' (Sir
John Suckling, 'Loving and Beloved')

'Every pelting, petty officer.'
(*Measure for Measure*, II, 2 (naval novel)).

For an artist significant experiences should be got over as soon as possible in life, so that they may be turned into art.

'Here lurks no treason, here no envy swells,
Here grow no damnèd drugs, here are no storms.'
(*Titus Andronicus*, I, 1)

A good book demands a good index but a good index redeems even an indifferent book.

Miscellaneous Verdicts
Assorted Estimates
Under Review   } titles for anthology
About Books
Critical Prospects
Assessments

When Dostoevsky was tied to a stake, blindfolded, waiting for execution, he heard the drums beating retreat. Having been in the Army he knew he was not going to be shot. If he had heard Reveille he would have known that he had been shot.

Reg Butler's girls are bony,
Where chill the wind moans
While those of Annigoni
Have academic tones.

A retired social climber.

Man Traps for Womanizers (title for a book of short stories).